YEARS

SIMON &
SCHUSTER
PAPERBACKS

WALK THROUGH FIRE

Sheila Johnson

with Lisa Dickey

SIMON & SCHUSTER PAPERBACKS

New York   London   Toronto   Sydney   New Delhi

An Imprint of Simon & Schuster, LLC
1230 Avenue of the Americas
New York, NY 10020

First Simon & Schuster trade paperback edition September 2024

SIMON & SCHUSTER PAPERBACKS and colophon are
registered trademarks of Simon & Schuster, LLC

Simon & Schuster: Celebrating 100 Years of Publishing in 2024

For information about special discounts for bulk purchases,
please contact Simon & Schuster Special Sales
at 1-866-506-1949 or business@simonandschuster.com.

The lyrics on page 53 are from Tevye's Dream from *Fiddler on the Roof*

The Simon & Schuster Speakers Bureau can bring authors to your live event.
For more information or to book an event, contact the
Simon & Schuster Speakers Bureau at 1-866-248-3049 or
visit our website at www.simonspeakers.com.

Interior design by Ruth Lee-Mui

Manufactured in the United States of America

1   3   5   7   9   10   8   6   4   2

Library of Congress Cataloging-in-Publication Data is available on file.

ISBN 978-1-6680-0713-6
ISBN 978-1-6680-0714-3 (pbk)
ISBN 978-1-6680-0715-0 (ebook)

For all the women who've walked through fire
and lived to tell about it

Contents

WALK
THROUGH
FIRE

PROLOGUE

The minute I open the front door of our house, I hear my brother's voice.

"Sheila! Come here!" he's shouting. "Something's wrong with Mom!" I drop my bag and coat and rush toward the kitchen. Having just finished a shift mopping floors at the J. C. Penney in downtown Maywood, Illinois, and a full day of high school before that, I'm worn out. But my brother, George Peter—G. P. for short—is only thirteen, and the sound of fear in his voice gets my legs moving.

I burst into the kitchen, where an unimaginable scene awaits. My mother is curled up on the floor, wailing in pain. Her eyes are glassy and blank, and her body shakes with what seems like convulsions. "Mom!" I say, dropping to my knees to bring my face close to hers. "What's going on?" She tries to speak but can't form words, her breath coming in ragged gasps. And then she starts wailing again, an otherworldly sound that echoes through the room that, until recently, was always the sanctuary of our home.

Day or night, I always loved being in our kitchen. Everything happened there; it was the heart of the house. Mom would be at the stove, pots bubbling, while friends from the block sat at the turquoise Formica table and gossiped. We had a porch that led out into the backyard, and on any given night a handful of neighbors might drop by for a drink and some conversation. A couple of years earlier I had planted morning glories, and those pretty purple flowers lent their sweet scent to the smells of my mother's cooking. Our kitchen had always been a cocoon, a place of comfort. A place where our family came together.

But just three weeks earlier, it had become something very different. It had become the place where our once happy family exploded.

I'd heard my parents arguing one night after dinner, and when I walked into the kitchen to see what the fuss was about, I could tell my mom had been crying. Her eyes were rimmed with red and her lips were tightly pursed, but when I looked from her to my father, he just stood there with a blank face, like he hadn't a care in the world. "I'm leaving," he announced to my brother and me. And that was how I learned that after eighteen years of marriage, after raising two children and buying a home and achieving what certainly looked like the American Dream, my father had decided he wanted something different out of life. As it turned out, that "something different" was running off with a nurse he'd met at the Veterans Administration hospital where he worked.

I was sixteen when my father announced he was leaving. I didn't know what infidelity was, and even if I had, I'd never have imagined he would commit it. Divorce was something that happened in books, not in my family. I had never heard my mom and dad arguing, had never seen a hint of conflict. But all of a sudden, here he was in the kitchen telling us, "I've got somebody else"—as if that explained anything at all. I screamed at him, told him I would never forgive him, called him names he probably had no idea I knew. He just turned and walked out, without even a backward glance.

At first, I thought he'd come back to us, because how could this possibly be happening? But after a few days, I understood that he was really gone. So I stormed up to my parents' bedroom, angrily stuffed all his clothes into whatever bags I could find, then threw them out onto the sidewalk.

When my father left, he took a chunk of my mother's heart with him. But he stole more than that from our family. He took away our trust, our sense of well-being—and our financial security. In 1965, divorce laws weren't kind to women like my mother. Even though my father was the one who'd cheated and broken up our family, he was under no obligation to support us financially, and my mother couldn't get a loan or even a credit card without his signature. I had been planning to go to college, but how could we afford it now? Forget about tuition and textbooks next year; without Dad's salary, we couldn't even afford to feed ourselves this week.

"Let him leave," my mother said bitterly. "We can hold this house down." I wasn't so sure about that. But I knew that in order for us to have a chance, I'd have to go to work. And so I went out and found a couple of part-time jobs, including the one at the J. C. Penney, where my job was to clean up the soda bar.

For three weeks, Mom, G. P., and I tried to find our footing as a newly broken family. I kept my head down, studying and working and trying not to think about the shock of what my father had done. I tried to talk logically with my mother about how we were going to make ends meet, but she couldn't face what was happening. She was still raw, and short-tempered enough that she'd take a hairbrush to my backside if I asked too many questions. Mom was angry, and because Dad was gone, she shifted that anger to my brother and me. Her soul was on fire with the pain of his betrayal.

And then, that night in the kitchen, she collapsed.

"Mom!" I shout, panic rising in my throat. "What's happening? What should I do?" Is my mother having a seizure? Is she dying? Terrified, I lunge for the phone on the wall and call for an ambulance. Then I dial the only other person I can think of, my aunt Mercedes. She's not my aunt by blood, but she's my godmother and my mom's best friend. And because Mom has no siblings, and we haven't heard a peep from my father since he walked out, she's the closest thing to family we're going to find.

The ambulance arrives quickly, and the EMTs start working on my mom. As they're getting her stabilized, one of them turns to me and says, "We'll take her in. But you know that's going to cost you eighty-five dollars, right?"

Wait—*what*? You have to *pay* for an ambulance to take someone to the hospital? Where am I going to get that kind of money? My brother and I are kids, my mother is incapacitated, and I don't know the first thing about how the adult world works. Will I get in trouble if I can't pay? What will happen if there are big hospital bills too? Does my mother even have health insurance? I don't know the answers to any of these questions. I'm just a sheltered high school student who, up until three weeks ago, spent my days blissfully studying, practicing cheerleading routines, and playing my violin. My biggest problem was figuring out which skirt and sweater to wear to school.

But in this moment, I realize with a shock that we could slide into a hole so deep we might never get back out.

This is the moment my childhood ended, with a stab of fear and panic that pierced right through me. Even now, if I close my eyes and think about it, I can still summon that awful feeling. It imprinted itself on me that day.

I stand there looking at that EMT, my mind racing and words failing to come. And then I hear a voice behind me. "I'll take care of it, Sheila. Come on, let's get in the car." It's Aunt Mercedes. Thank god I called her, because she arrives just in time to pull me back from the brink. As the EMTs load my mother onto a stretcher, Aunt Mercedes leads G. P. and me to her car and then drives us behind the ambulance to the emergency room.

The doctors admit my mom into the hospital, where she stays for several days to be treated for a "nervous breakdown." I don't really understand what that means, but I know it's happening because of my father's betrayal. Mom loves a man who has wounded her without care or concern, and I have seen it nearly destroy her. *No man is worth this*, I think. That feeling only intensifies when I call my father to tell him what has happened.

"Mom had a breakdown," I say. "She's in the hospital." The ramifications should be obvious to him: He has two young teenagers who are home alone. Our mother is sick. We're scared. He needs to take care of us, or at the very least offer us some words of comfort.

Instead, what he says is, "That is *not* my problem."

I can't believe what I'm hearing. My father's reaction is so cold, so unfeeling. He doesn't care what's happening to my mother, his wife of nearly two decades. And he doesn't care what's happening to G. P. and me. In that moment, I vow that I will never be in the position my mother has found herself in—dependent on a man for her sense of self-worth, for her financial security, for the support of her children.

I swear it to myself that day. I am determined. I believe it.

But you know what they say about the best-laid plans, don't you? Ironically enough, my fierce determination not to end up like my mother put me on a path that took me straight there. I wouldn't see this for years, blinded as I was by love, loyalty, and a whole lot of naïveté. But the shock and fear that flooded my soul in the kitchen that day would color everything that came after in my life: My thirty-three-year marriage to Bob Johnson. My feelings about money and security. My relationships with other people, my work, and my family. Even my sense of self. And my eyes didn't truly open to all of this until it was almost too late.

These days, I'm a successful businesswoman, a happy wife, a mother and grandmother. It might look from the outside like I had it easy, riding the rise of Black Entertainment Television to a life of wealth and privilege. But believe me when I tell you, I had to walk through fire to get here. And after many years of staying silent, I'm ready to reveal how it all went down, in hopes that my story might help other women who find themselves facing the fire too.

I'LL CATCH YOU

It's Friday night in the Rust Belt town of Monessen, Pennsylvania. I'm sitting in front of our family's new DuMont television set with its rabbit-ear antennas, eating a TV dinner from a tray and watching *Howdy Doody*, my favorite show. I like watching TV in our little living room, but even at age four, I can smell the dankness of our apartment and this town. Monessen is a blue-collar suburb of Pittsburgh, and at this time, in 1953, it's full of steelworkers and the bars and gambling halls they like to frequent.

Suddenly, there's a pounding at our door. My father opens it to find a young man, his head bleeding, asking for help sewing up the wound. It's a steel mill worker who's been in a bar fight, and someone told him there's a doctor living in the apartment above the barbershop. My father invites him in, then washes his hands and stitches up the gash, no questions asked. And I just keep on watching *Howdy Doody*, because even as a child, I have seen that this is the kind of thing that happens on weekends in Monessen.

That's my earliest memory, and it features my father doing what he did best. Dr. George P. Crump was a calm and capable physician, educated at two historically Black universities—Lincoln in Pennsylvania for undergraduate, then Howard University for medical school—and one of a very small handful of African American neurosurgeons in the country at that time. Despite our modest apartment in Monessen, we were an upper-middle-class family, with my father working as a doctor and my mother as an accountant. Yet even though both worked white-collar jobs, Black professionals still got paid only a fraction of what white people got paid for the same positions, no matter their skill level.

My father had a genius-level intellect but an awkward social manner, often making strange little jokes that made sense in his own mind but fell flat in company. Once, when a fellow doctor greeted him at the hospital with "Hello, Dr. Crump. How's your day?" he answered, "Two psychiatrists meet in a hallway. One says to the other, 'Hello!' And the other thinks, *I wonder what he meant by that?*" And then he laughed at his own joke and kept on walking past his confused colleague.

Dad was a little weird, in the way brilliant people sometimes are. One night, he brought home a big jar of formaldehyde with a wrinkled blob floating inside. He had lost a patient on the operating table, and he was so upset that he decided to bring the brain home, to poke around and see if he could figure out what had gone wrong. The smell was horrible, but Dad didn't seem to notice, even when Mom put her hands on her hips and said, "Really, George? You couldn't have done this at the hospital?" He just sat at the kitchen table, picking at this rubbery-looking thing, until he finally said, "Aha!" He had located a small tumor he'd missed in the operating room.

While Dad was cerebral and reserved, Mom was chatty and warm. Marie Iris Crump was petite and pretty, and she was always smiling and cracking jokes, trying to make people laugh. She could talk to absolutely anyone, and she loved to entertain. On Saturdays, she'd cook all day, making everything from scratch, and then she'd serve a huge meal on Sunday for anybody who felt like coming by. Mom was a generous soul, happy to feed the whole neighborhood with her homemade sausage, fried chicken, and pies.

Unlike Dad, who preferred to spend his free time with his nose buried in medical books, Mom liked socializing with friends. She loved parties and often had a group of ladies over for all-night bridge sessions. Once, when my father overheard some of their in-game chitchat, he felt the need to confront my mother about it. "Why do you call each other names?" he asked her. "It just seems rude."

"George," she said, laughing, "we're talking about 'dummy' hands. It's part of the game."

My parents were opposites in how they looked too. Mom was dark skinned and slender, with an open face and big smile. Dad, who was one-quarter Sicilian, was very light skinned, with wavy hair and green eyes. He wasn't athletic at all, being five foot seven and a little thick around the middle, but he adored the arts and music. Both my parents played piano, but my father had a natural gift for it. While some doctors would hit the bar after a long day of surgery, he'd come home and hit the piano. He would sit there playing for hours, sometimes not even bothering to change out of his blood-flecked white lab coat. The music calmed his mind.

Dad often took us to concerts and the theater, and he also liked to bring me to work with him, sometimes even letting me watch as he performed surgeries. To my embarrassment and delight, he would brag about me to his colleagues, and he urged me to study hard so I could follow in his footsteps. "Pay attention, Sheila," he'd say, "and one day, just like me, you'll be carving into someone's skull." I looked up to this man, a doctor whose own father had worked on the railroad and whose grandfather was the son of enslaved people. And I was his favored child, the apple of his eye—which was another reason why his leaving turned me inside out.

Our family life had always been predictable and steady, except for one particular part of my father's career. Many hospitals wouldn't even think of hiring Black doctors, because white patients would refuse to be seen by them. Dad worked for Veterans Administration hospitals, because those were the only ones that would hire him. And even then, he had to move from job to job, because none of the VA hospitals would give him a contract for more than a few months.

We moved thirteen times before I turned ten. My mother never complained, but I know it had to have been hard on her. I didn't mind it, though. Each time we moved, it felt like an adventure, a chance to make new friends and reinvent myself. I learned how to adjust quickly to new environments and how to talk to all different kinds of people. I also learned some hard lessons about race.

When I was about six years old, we moved to Erie, Pennsylvania. There was a white family down the block with a girl about my age, so I rode my tricycle to her house and we started playing in the yard with a couple of other neighborhood kids—this was in the days when kids would play outside all day long, coming in only when their parents called them in for dinner. But suddenly, this girl's mother came running out the front door, yelling at her daughter to come inside. When I asked why she had to go, her mom said, "Because you are as black as a brick."

I'm what, now? I looked at my arm, which wasn't black at all, but more of a light tan color, like my father's skin. What did the lady mean? Confused, I rode my tricycle home and told my mom what had happened. "You're not literally black, honey," she said. "What she meant was, you're a Negro." This just confused me further. "Don't worry," Mom said. "I'll take care of it." She went down the street to talk to the other mom, but it didn't do any good. That was the last time I got to play with that girl.

I hardly had time to be sad, though, because soon enough we moved again, giving me the opportunity to start fresh somewhere else. We left Pennsylvania for Louisville, Kentucky, settling on a street not far from a cemetery. I probably wouldn't even have re-membered that detail, except for the fact that the Black kids in our neighborhood had to walk through the cemetery to get to their ele-mentary school. Even though the Supreme Court's *Brown v. Board of Education* decision had recently declared racial segregation uncon-stitutional, the schools there were still divided by color.

When my father learned that I'd have to walk through the cem-etery to school, he said, "No, we're not doing that." Instead, he en-rolled me in the second grade—with all the moving around, I had managed to skip ahead a year—at a nearby white elementary school. Because I was so fair skinned, with straight hair that I pulled into a braided ponytail, I could pass for white. My father, with his green eyes and light skin, could too. We just had to hide my mother, never having her pick me up at school or come to any events there.

I knew we were pulling a con, and I loved it. And my father seemed pretty pleased about it too. Not only did he not want me walking through a cemetery, he knew the white school was better academically. And he no doubt had some residual feelings about how he was being treated as a Black doctor, being shunted all over the country. Sneaking me into that school must have felt like a nice little poke in the eye to the white society that rejected him.

What made it even sweeter was the fact that when Dad told my teacher he was a doctor, she decided to designate me our class nurse. This meant that whenever one of my classmates got hurt, it was my job to clean the wound and put a Band-Aid on it. I remember how proud I was to have special access to the first aid kit, and of course my father loved that I was practicing to become a doctor. But the best part was that all that time, these white kids had a little Black girl treating them, touching their skin and rubbing ointment into their bruises, and while their parents would have gone crazy if they'd known, they never did find out. We managed to keep our secret the whole of my second-grade year. And then, of course, we moved again.

It wasn't just the uprooting that was hard on my mother. It was also the difficulty of physically getting us from one place to another. These were the days when Black people couldn't just stop at any roadside diner, hotel, or restaurant, because many were for whites only. The *Green Book*—or as it's actually titled, *The Negro Motorist Green Book*—was our guide to where we could eat or stay, but in many states such places were few and far between. So my mother had to spend the whole day before each move frying up chickens, making sandwiches, and baking cakes, then packing it all into picnic baskets and coolers for the road.

Sometimes, we'd just pull off the highway and eat in the car. And then we'd hustle off behind a tree or a bush to pee, because there was no telling how far we'd have to go before finding a Negro-friendly restroom. My parents tried to use these times to educate G. P. and me about discrimination, but for us kids, being on the road just felt like another adventure. By the time we got to Maywood, Illinois, in 1959, though, my mom had had more than enough of such "adventures."

"We have got to settle somewhere," she told my father. "You have to find a way." And finally, somehow, he did. After all the moves and uncertainty of the previous ten years, my father managed to land a permanent position at the Edward Hines Jr. VA Hospital in Hines, Illinois, just outside Chicago. We settled in the small town of Maywood, and that's where I lived from ages nine to seventeen, when I graduated from high school.

I was getting ready to start fifth grade at Irving Elementary when the school district sent a note home to all the parents. As part of a push to get students involved in the arts, the district was offering music lessons, including a free instrument, to any student who wanted to learn. So, at age nine, I just had to choose which instrument I wanted to play.

Because my parents were both pianists, they had started me on piano lessons when I was in kindergarten. I had discovered I hated playing the piano, mostly because I hated my piano teacher, Mrs. Watts. She was an older woman with incredibly stinky breath, and she liked to rap my little knuckles with a ruler whenever I played a wrong note. Every week, I dreaded going to my piano lesson, so when it came time to choose an instrument for the District 89 Orchestra, I was determined to go in another direction.

"I want to play the violin," I told my parents.

"Why violin?" my father asked. Honestly, I didn't know. There was just something about the instrument that intrigued me. Whenever my father took me to orchestra performances, I found myself watching the first-chair violinist, awed by the grace of movement that produced such gorgeous sounds. I thought it might feel nice to play an instrument I could cradle and hold close to me. And so that's what I asked for—not having any idea that from the moment I picked up a violin, I would fall in love.

I still remember opening the case for the first time, inhaling the sweet smell of spruce wood and velvet that came wafting out. I carefully picked up the violin, feeling the smoothness of the neck, then ran my fingers over the elegant f-shaped holes in the body. I thought this was the most beautiful instrument I had ever seen, and I couldn't wait to learn how to play it.

Unlike stinky Mrs. Watts, my first violin teacher was encouraging and kind. He taught me how to hold the bow, explaining that the hairs were from horses' tails. He showed me how to cradle the violin under my chin, then warned, "You've chosen one of the hardest instruments, so be patient. It's going to take a while to learn." I suppose he was worried I'd get discouraged, because it truly is difficult for a beginning violinist to make much more than a squawking noise. But from the moment I laid my bow on the strings, I couldn't get enough.

I started playing for hours every day. In contrast to the piano lessons, which my parents had to drag me to, I couldn't wait for my violin lessons. I wanted to learn everything, to be able to create the kinds of sounds I'd heard in the orchestras my father had taken me to hear. Whenever my teacher gave me a pointer or new skill to learn, I practiced relentlessly until I could do it. There was something almost spiritual about this process, as if the violin were becoming a part of me.

And there was another reason I loved it: playing in the orchestra also brought me out of my shell.

I was a quiet kid, just a different egg from the rest of my class-mates. I wasn't shy, exactly, but I was awkward and a little bit inse-cure. Even though I hadn't minded all that moving around during my childhood, it had kept me from forming deep bonds with friends. So, while I had no problem talking to kids my age, I never ended up feeling very close to any of them. I was lonely, and the loneliness it-self compounded the problem, marking me as an oddball in the eyes of my peers.

Music became my security blanket and the orchestra my com-fort zone. The best thing about making music in a group of people is that everyone is engaged in a common pursuit. In the orchestra, we relied on each other to bring a piece of music to life, and we learned quickly that it worked only when we were giving and taking and paying attention to each other. Playing in an orchestra teaches you how to listen. It teaches you empathy. And it makes you feel part of something bigger than yourself.

I remember the power of feeling those sounds swell around me—the cello, the viola, the horns, the woodwinds, the timpani. It felt like magic, seeing a conductor take a couple dozen squirming elementary school kids and turn them into a single entity. And because of the free-instruments policy, the district had almost 100 percent partic-ipation from the students. Even if a student couldn't figure out the french horn or the oboe, they would be in the back tinging wildly away on a triangle. We had orchestra practice every day, and each morning I'd wake up eager to make music and learn something new.

When my family first moved to Maywood, we rented an apart-ment on the second floor of a town house. But once my father knew that his position at the Hines VA hospital would be permanent, he bought us a house at 237 South Twentieth Avenue, in a mostly Black middle-class neighborhood with emerald-green lawns and wide sidewalks.

Our house was tall and narrow, two stories plus a converted attic, with a classic suburban clapboard exterior and a peaked roof. It had four small bedrooms, which felt luxurious for our family of four, but it had only one bathroom, which drove me crazy, particularly as I got older. I just hated following anyone into the bathroom, so I made sure to get up earlier than everyone to be the first in there to do my business.

Apart from that, though, I loved our house—especially my bedroom, which had bunk beds, a little desk, and my prized possession, an old-fashioned phonograph. My mom bought me all kinds of records, from classical music to Motown, and I'd spend hours listening in my room. I felt so fancy sliding a vinyl disk out of its sleeve, putting it on my record player, then dropping the needle into the groove. My room was my cocoon, and in the hours I spent in there studying and practicing my violin, I felt like a lucky little girl.

Maybe it's because these years were so good that I still remember one event in particular that wasn't. It happened one night when I was in the eighth grade. As I was lying on my top bunk reading and listening to music, my father walked into my room.

"Time for dinner, Sheila," he said.

"Okay, coming," I replied. Ever the dutiful child, I started to put my book away and climb down the little ladder.

"Just jump, I'll catch you," Dad said, stretching his arms toward me. He'd never suggested such a thing before, so I was excited. I threw myself off the bunk, grinning from ear to ear—and then *smack*!

I hit the floor, hard. Confused, with the wind knocked out of me, I looked up at him.

"That's a lesson," my father said. "Don't trust anybody."

I started crying. "I trusted *you*," I said. But he just turned and walked out of the room.

I wonder now whether he had already started messing around with that nurse, and whether this was his way of trying to prepare me for the heartbreak that was coming. I never asked him, so I'll never know. At the time, I decided just to push away my hurt feelings and go on like nothing had happened. This was the first time I did that—but it was far from the last time.

Two

PERPETUAL MOTION

I'm standing onstage with the orchestra at Proviso East High School, preparing to play my first solo. I'm thirteen years old, though I look younger, with my hair pulled back and dressed in my military-style orchestra jacket and black pants.

It's been four years since I started playing the violin, and the fingertips on my left hand have grown hard with calluses from pressing the strings. Since the moment I first picked up the instrument, I've practiced every day until my fingers throbbed, trying to perfect my scales, bow technique, phrasing—all the elements that turn a good violinist into a great one. I'm not there yet, but being invited to solo makes it feel like I'm on the right track.

And yet . . . I'm so nervous right now, I can barely hold my bow. My whole body is shaking as I step to the front of the orchestra, so I take a couple of deep breaths, trying to calm myself. Luckily for me, the piece I'm playing—a movement called "Perpetual Motion," from a suite by the German composer Carl Bohm—sets off like a house on fire and never lets up. I launch into my solo, my fingers flying up and down the violin's neck and my bow hand a blur. Once I've started, there's no time to think, which means there's no time to stay nervous.

Something takes over, and suddenly, it's just me and the violin. I lose myself in the music, and when I finish the solo, I look up in amazement to see the audience on its feet, cheering for me with a full-on standing ovation. Behind me, the other string players in the orchestra tap their music stands with their bows, a show of appreciation and respect that almost brings me to tears. I feel overwhelmed, filled with a kind of contentment I've never known before.

It was just a school concert, of course, not a performance at Carnegie Hall. But this would turn out to be a touchstone moment in my life, my first time accomplishing something difficult that I wasn't sure I could do. The insecurity that permeated my day-to-day existence seemed to evaporate when I lost myself in that piece, and I felt a new kind of confidence. Throughout my childhood, I had a strange habit of constantly asking myself, *Why am I here?* In that moment, I began to see the answer. Playing that solo centered me inside myself. It made me realize I could make a career out of music, and so I decided to set my mind to making that happen.

For as much as I had been practicing, I pushed myself to do even more. I turned into a dervish at home, playing and playing until my mother finally said, "Sheila, *enough!*" I was driving the whole family crazy, so to give them a few hours of peace, I started a new practice routine. I'd do all my homework right after school, then take a quick nap in the early evening. We'd have dinner as a family, and then I'd go to sleep for another few hours. I would set my alarm for midnight, and when everyone else was dead asleep, I'd sneak down to the kitchen and practice my violin. I loved playing in the kitchen, which had the best acoustics in the house, and somehow, my parents and G. P. managed to sleep through it.

I asked for private lessons in addition to my school instruction, so my mother signed me up to study with the orchestra director Sidney Miller at the Fine Arts Building, a former carriage factory in downtown Chicago that had been turned into a thriving creative center, with music rehearsal rooms, dance studios, and auditoriums. Every Monday I'd walk in through the ornate arched doorway, squeeze into a hand-crank elevator operated by an older man wearing a uniform, and listen to the sounds of music wafting in as we rose through the building. I'd study with Mr. Miller for an hour, and then, after my lesson, Mom would take me to the Artist's Café downstairs for dinner. I loved everything about those Monday nights, which made me feel like part of a grand artistic tradition.

My parents were completely supportive of my musical pursuits, and even as a young person I knew how lucky that was. Too often in the African American community, kids aren't raised with the message that they can do anything they set their minds to. There's no sense of wonder, of flowering, because the message to children has historically been, "You should be seen but not heard." I don't mean to blame Black families, as there are deeply rooted historical and cultural reasons why that attitude evolved. But later in life, I couldn't help but compare it with the kind of support that some other groups offer their gifted, talented, and creative kids.

Yet George and Marie Crump not only talked the talk, they walked the walk. When my mother saw how determined I was to pursue a career in music, she persuaded my father to buy me an eighteenth-century violin made by the master Italian luthier Carlo

Ferdinando Landolfi. They had to take out a second mortgage on the house, as the violin cost about $15,000, which was an absolute fortune back then. But my mom believed I needed to have a first-class instrument to achieve my goal of making a life in music.

For me, the Landolfi was more than just a violin; it represented my parents' belief in my abilities. Having that precious instrument made me want to work even harder, to fulfill not only my own dreams but the dreams they had for me. When I first held it in my hands, I thought I would own and cherish it forever. And I would have, too, if it weren't for the way things unfolded over the next decade and a half.

For the most part, I enjoyed my high school years. I loved playing in the orchestra, of course, and I also joined the cheerleading squad, even getting the nickname "Jelly Hips" when I introduced a few new steps to the routines of my mostly white team. I became friends with some of the boys on the football team, primarily because my mom was always inviting them over for pancake breakfasts or hamburger nights. Mom turned our house into a social hub, and there were always people coming and going.

Yet I still felt that same lingering loneliness as I had in elementary school. Some of the kids called me "high yellow," because I was the light-skinned daughter of a doctor. I had long, straight hair and fair skin, and one Black girl in my class just seemed to hate me for it. She'd wait for me down by the underpass beneath Washington Boulevard, then beat the crap out of me as I was walking home from school. My freshman and sophomore years in particular, I didn't feel like I fit in with the Black community or the white community. I was in this strange limbo.

I also didn't get along with the Proviso orchestra teacher in those years. His name was Mr. Leinhart, and for whatever reason, he just seemed to have a stick up his butt when it came to me. He never said anything disparaging directly to me, but no matter how hard I worked or how well I played, he would not advance me to first chair. So I was relieved when, at the beginning of my junior year, he was replaced by a young woman, a freshly minted music teacher who'd recently graduated from the University of Illinois.

Susan Starrett was just twenty-four, not much older than some of her students, but she blew into Proviso with the skills and confidence of an old pro. Having grown up in Peoria, she had a Midwestern openness about her, but she also didn't brook any foolishness. She could be strict, but only because she cared about turning us into better musicians and stronger people. During my last two years of high school, I learned a lot about music from her, but I also learned life skills. She became my mentor, teaching me how to focus, how to be resilient, how to set goals and take deliberate steps toward achieving them. These skills became the foundation for the way I approach life—even today, more than six decades later.

At age fifteen, I had never bonded with a peer in the way I bonded with Susan. I never knew for sure what other girls thought of me, but I trusted Susan completely. She earned that trust early on, when she revealed to me that my instincts about Mr. Leinhart had been correct.

While looking through some student records during her first year at Proviso, she came across a write-up Mr. Leinhart had done about me. He called me "boy crazy" (even though I hadn't really dated anybody yet), criticized me for being a cheerleader, and suggested that, because I was "all over the place," I didn't have much of a future ahead of me. After a few months as my teacher, having seen how wrong Mr. Leinhart's assessment was, Susan decided to show me what he'd written. This was against school rules, which only made me appreciate Susan more. I thought, *This woman is okay*.

Susan got to know my family, too, and my parents loved her. Sometimes, after a late rehearsal, she'd give me a lift home. My mom would invite her in for something to eat, or at the very least she'd send her home with a Tupperware container full of food. A couple of times, Susan mentioned seeing my dad at Petersen's Ice Cream parlor in downtown Maywood, sitting alone. This seemed strange to me; what was Dad doing having a meal by himself there? Did he not want to have dinner with his family? I couldn't figure it out—until that terrible night during my junior year of high school, when my dad told my mom he was leaving.

I didn't go to school the day after my dad walked out. I just couldn't; my whole world felt shattered. It was very unusual for me to miss school, so Susan called the house, and when I told her what had happened, she came to check on me. She was incredibly supportive, not just of me but of my mother too. Susan was one of two women, the other being Aunt Mercedes, who checked in regularly and helped us to keep moving forward, step by step, day by day.

This was particularly hard for my mother to do, because from the moment my father left, she felt like a failure. She was paralyzed by guilt that she hadn't been able to keep her family together. What kind of wife can't hold on to her man? What kind of mother lets the father of her children walk out of their lives? Because that's what my father did: He didn't just walk out for show, then visit G. P. and me on weekends and call us on our birthdays. No, he moved in with the nurse, and that was that—it was like we didn't even exist anymore. I saw him only once more in my entire life, and that was by accident.

It happened a few years after he'd left. His brother, my beloved uncle Joe, was dying of stomach cancer. I drove to the hospital to see him, and when I walked into his room, there sat my father. I just stared for a moment, too shocked to speak. I don't remember exactly what he said, but I do remember that he started berating me for the Christmas gifts I had sent him. Because yes, even though he had abandoned my brother and me, even though we never heard another word from him, I had sent him a couple of books I thought he'd like. No matter how badly he had treated us, I still wanted to please him. But now, here he was, taking a precious moment in his dying brother's hospital room—a moment in which he could have tried to mend our relationship—to criticize me for the gifts I'd sent.

All I could think was, *Why is he doing this to me?* Why had this man, who had for so long been such a proud and attentive father, turned so utterly cold? I drove myself crazy trying to figure out what I had done wrong, but eventually, after years of agonizing, I would come to realize that his transformation had nothing to do with me. As brilliant as my father was intellectually, I believe he was stunted emotionally. There was something soft and weak about him, and whether he abandoned his family of his own volition or because the nurse he ran away with wanted him to, it was the act of a weak person.

When I think of him now, I remember an incident that happened in Chicago. We had driven into the city to take my mom out for Mother's Day, and my dad rolled through a stop sign. Sure enough, the blue lights came flashing, and a police car pulled him over. When the officer walked up to the driver's-side window, my dad—neurosurgeon, accomplished pianist, the person I looked up to most in the world—just became this mealymouthed, spineless blob. His voice must have gone up two octaves as he talked to that policeman. Now, I understand that Black people in this country, and particularly Black men, have to be careful around the police. With his pale skin and green eyes, Dad could pass for white, but he had the rest of us in the car, so maybe that made him nervous. But all that aside, there was just something about the way my father crumbled in that moment that felt uncomfortable to me. He seemed to lack a backbone. And that's how I think of him today.

Yet as weak as he was, my father was still able to strike my mother a crippling blow just by leaving her. Mom had poured herself into that marriage, and into raising G. P. and me. Dad left for his own reasons, but to her way of thinking, it was because she wasn't good enough. What made it worse was the fact that this was the second time in her life she'd been made to feel that way.

The first time happened when my mother and father got married. As Mom was preparing the paperwork for the marriage license, she had to fill in the names of her parents. She'd grown up in Philadelphia, and from an early age she knew she was adopted. We used to spend summers with my grandparents in their row house on Walnut Street—they were the sweetest people, friendly to everyone, and we'd sit on their front porch and drink lemonade and chat with the neighbors. Mom had a great relationship with them. But somehow, in the process of doing this paperwork, she discovered that her parents never actually adopted her. She was a foster child.

This discovery rocked my mother's world. Why hadn't they adopted her? And why had they hidden that fact from her? Foster parents get a stipend from the state, and adoptive parents don't, so that might have been the reason. But all my mother could think was, *I wasn't good enough for them.* Surely, if they really loved her as their own, they'd have gone ahead and adopted her. Learning that they hadn't cut a deep wound into my mother's soul. Two decades later, my father's leaving tore that wound right back open.

The pain she felt was compounded by the fact that when Dad walked out, Mom instantly lost her status in the Black community. George and Marie Crump had been the picture of success for a mid-century African American family: a surgeon married to an accountant, two kids, nice house in the suburbs. I remember my mother's getting dressed up for medical convention dinners and awards nights at fancy hotels downtown. She would just beam when she walked out of the house on my father's arm, happy to take her rightful place among the cream of Black society.

When Dad left, my mother felt as if she'd been dropped off the face of the earth. There would be no more dinners, no more social gatherings. She was a wreck, not only unfit for company but also spending most of her time scrambling to make ends meet. She took a job doing accounting work and also started taking in boarders in our home. One night, I came home to find police cars surrounding our house, as it turned out one of our boarders was wanted on some kind of criminal charge. In a breathtakingly short period of time, we went from having a steady, stable home environment to feeling like the walls were coming down.

Through it all, I did the one thing that always brought me comfort. I just kept playing my violin—trying to make it to graduation, hoping my mother would bounce back, praying that life would somehow find its way back to normal.

· · ·

Even music, which had always been my refuge, turned into a roller-coaster ride during my senior year of high school.

Despite struggling with insecurity, I was an ambitious child, and every year I would audition for the Illinois All-State Orchestra. I'd been accepted a couple of times, but now I was determined not only to make the orchestra but to earn first-chair honors. All those hours of practice, all those midnight sessions in the kitchen, all that sweat and toil—it finally paid off when I made first chair in my senior year.

I had done it! I was officially the best high school violinist in the state. With everything our family had been through, I felt particularly proud and relieved to have reached such an important milestone. When I saw another violinist walking over, I smiled, assuming she was coming to congratulate me. Instead, she leaned close and said, "You know you only got it because you're a n——."

Anger surged through me. "I *earned* this!" I retorted. But that girl couldn't have cared less. She knew that simply saying those words was all it took to taint my accomplishment. I was one of very few Black string players, and I suppose it shouldn't have surprised me that kids like her wanted to protect their lily-white establishment. This was the mid-1960s, and she certainly wasn't the only one among the students—and, sadly, some teachers too—who didn't welcome the societal change that was bringing faces like mine into previously all-white spaces.

And that was another reason why I felt so lucky to have Susan Starrett as my mentor. She never saw me as a Black violinist; she just saw me as a young violinist with promise. When I had the honor of playing with the Chicago Civic Symphony, she took me to a nice restaurant to celebrate—and she used the opportunity to educate me on manners, how to dress and how to comport oneself in a formal environment. She understood that, with my father gone and my mother struggling, I needed someone to help me navigate the transition to adulthood. She truly wanted me to succeed, maybe even as much as I wanted to myself.

She also understood that I had some disadvantages when it came to getting into college. Even though my parents were both college graduates, they had gone to historically Black colleges and universities. Neither of them had ever talked to me about the possibility of going to college elsewhere, and they didn't know anything at all about requirements such as taking the Scholastic Aptitude Test, or SAT. I didn't even know what the SAT was until Susan told me about it, and at her insistence, I went ahead and signed up to take it.

In recent years, there's been a lot of discussion about whether the SAT is biased toward students from white and wealthy backgrounds. Those discussions weren't happening back when I took the test, but I can tell you this: I was a very good student, with excellent grades, but I absolutely tanked on the SAT. I had never taken an hours-long multiple-choice test, and many of the questions did not speak to my experience. My score was so low that when I showed it to Susan, she just looked at me in confusion. "This can't be right," she said. But it was. And now I wondered if I'd be able to get into college at all.

Susan urged me to apply to her alma mater, the University of Illinois, and she started reaching out to the administration on my behalf. She called Paul Rolland, a legendary violin teacher and her own mentor when she was at the university, to tell him about me. She also called Dan Perrino, the director of music extension and founder of the Illinois Summer Youth Music programs. These two men had been the heart and soul of Susan's musical education at Illinois, and she contacted them with a simple message. "You're going to teach this young lady," she told them. "We have got to find a way to get her into the university."

Susan did more than just get me into the University of Illinois—something I couldn't have done on my own with those SAT scores. She also helped me get a full four-year scholarship to study music. I had been under a huge amount of stress, working multiple jobs and just trying to make it through high school. Now I could head off to college with all my bills paid—room, board, and full tuition. I was ecstatic.

When I think back on high school, I can't believe how lucky I was that Susan Starrett walked into my life. Her dedication to my future success was unwavering and total, and even beyond our classroom relationship, we became real friends. I know it's unusual for teachers and students to form that kind of bond, but there was something special about our connection, right from the start.

There's one other memory that stands out for me from my senior year of high school. Our orchestra was scheduled to play an evening concert at Eureka College, a small school famous for being Ronald Reagan's alma mater, a couple of hours' drive from Maywood. On the day of the performance, Susan got the news that her father had died suddenly of a heart attack. She told me at school, her eyes welling with tears. But she made it clear that we would go ahead with the concert that evening.

Onstage that night, we made it through a couple of pieces. And then it was time to play a selection from Symphony no. 2 in D Major by the Finnish composer Jean Sibelius—a moving piece that the composer once described as "a confession of the soul." The second movement includes a violin solo, and as the first chair, I was to play it.

I rose to take my place next to the conductor's podium, and I could see that Susan was fighting to keep her composure. I just felt for her in that moment, seeing her struggle with her pain. In the brief time she and I had known each other, we had both lost our dads, albeit in very different ways. I wanted somehow to honor hers, so as she lifted her baton, I said, "I dedicate this to your father." She started to cry, which brought me to tears too. The entire orchestra rose to the occasion, and as the music swelled around me, I was swept up in the most emotion and power I'd ever felt onstage.

I couldn't have known it then, but the bond Susan and I developed during those years would last throughout our lives. In fact, we're still very close friends to this day. I would find other mentors during my college years, but she was my first and the one with whom I remained closest. And of course, she was the person who made it possible for me to go to college at all.

After graduation, as I prepared to head off to the University of Illinois, I was excited to make a fresh start. I had spent my last two years of high school under the cloud of my father's betrayal, and now I could finally get away from it. My mother was getting back on her feet, finding solace in her church and community of friends, and she was strong enough to take care of my brother, who appeared to be still struggling. For the first time in my life, I would have no one to answer to, and I could just focus on school, music, and my own life.

At least, that was the plan.

Three

FIST THROUGH THE WALL

It's the late summer of 1966, and my mother is dropping me off in the college town of Champaign-Urbana, three hours away from Maywood, to start this new, independent phase of my life. I've chosen all my classes and will be living in a dorm room with one other girl, but before that, I'm signed up for something called freshman camp. This is a one-week orientation for new students, and the university has randomly paired each freshman with a junior to introduce them to campus life.

Out of thousands of juniors at the University of Illinois that year, the one I just happen to get paired with is a guy named Robert L. Johnson.

I don't remember my first impression of Bob, probably because nothing about him particularly stood out. He was short, about five foot seven, and darker skinned than me. I didn't think he was particularly handsome, though he had a nice smile. What I do remember is that, from the moment he introduced himself, he never really left my side. He stuck to me like glue that week, whether we were playing those silly little icebreaker games with the group, sitting around a campfire, or walking across the campus. Bob decided he liked me, and that was that. He was going to make me his girl.

Up to that point, I'd had only one boyfriend. His name was Thomas Les Purce, and I was crazy about him. He didn't actually live in Maywood, but he had an aunt who did, and so he spent summers there. He and I got to know each other during those times, and we started dating even though he lived in Pocatello, Idaho. We had gotten serious enough that he'd flown in for prom my senior year of high school, and when I graduated, we still considered ourselves a couple.

Tom was everything I could have wanted in a boyfriend. He was smart, handsome, and thoughtful, and he was the perfect gentleman. I was friends with a lot of the boys in my high school, and none of them could compare to him. But when he enrolled at Idaho State University, we realized it didn't make sense to try to stay a couple. We were just too young, and we both understood that long-distance college relationships don't have much of a chance. Deep down, though, there was a part of me that wished we had tried to keep the relationship going. I loved Tom, and I felt safe with him. There would be many times over the coming years that I found myself wishing he and I had stayed together.

When Bob Johnson set his sights on me, I felt flattered. He was three years older than me (though just two years ahead in school) and a member of the Kappa Alpha Psi fraternity, and while I had no interest in joining the Greek system myself, that provided me an instant connection to a social life. He just kept calling to ask me out, and within the first few weeks of school he was taking me to parties and introducing me to his fraternity brothers as his girlfriend. I was excited to be invited into a group of smart, ambitious Black students—the first time I felt like part of an elite slice of Black society. Bob was my connection into that world.

Bob was charming, and he could sweet-talk anybody. He was smart and enormously ambitious, and I hadn't seen that combination in many of the young men I knew. And he was very attentive to me, which I liked. He was always at my side—except when there was dancing at the parties. He didn't like to dance, but I did. I'd get out on the floor and shake my "jelly hips," and when I'd had enough, he was right there, ready to take my arm again.

As everyone does, he and I brought the burdens of our backgrounds to the relationship. I still felt a void from my father's leaving, and it felt good to have a man who wanted to be with me all the time. Bob's baggage was different. He was the ninth of ten children, born in the tiny town of Hickory, Mississippi, into a poor farming family. Bob knew what it felt like to be judged for where he'd come from, and he was determined to get as far away from that as he could in his adult life. Going out with the daughter of a doctor—even though that doctor had abandoned his family—probably helped make him feel like a big man. I didn't realize it at the time, because he was incredibly good at hiding things, but apparently Bob's insecurities ran very deep.

In the beginning, at least, each of us filled a need the other had. I was charmed by Bob's insistence on always being at my side, even when that insistence felt possessive. I told myself that he was only behaving this way because he cared for me so much—and wasn't that what I wanted? Someone who would stay, rather than leave as my father had?

Aside from my high school relationship with Tom, I had no real experience with men. I was just seventeen when Bob and I started dating, and in many ways I was still a girl. Maybe because Tom had been so good to me, I readily gave Bob the same kind of trust I had given him. I believed Bob was devoted to me and would be honest with me. So in the middle of my freshman year, when I discovered that one of my favorite record albums had gone missing—I think it was the Broadway cast recording of *West Side Story*—there was no reason for me to suspect that he'd given it to another woman. But that's what had happened. I can't remember how I found out, but when I approached Bob about it, he made me feel like a fool for even asking. He was testing me, trying to see if he could get away with it. And he did, of course, because I either believed him or chose to forgive him. Maybe a little of both.

That was the first red flag, and it started flying even before Christmas break. Just as in high school, I didn't have any close female friends, so if I had been inclined to talk to a girlfriend about what was going on, I wouldn't have known where to turn. And strangely enough, I didn't even have a roommate to talk to. At the end of my first week of college, the other girl in my room—a blond freshman named Lynn—simply disappeared. I don't know if she dropped out, ran away with a guy, or what, but her mom kept calling our room that week, and all I could say was, "Maybe she's in the library"—because that's where I would have been. I have no idea what happened to her, but the result was that I ended up with a room of my own.

Which meant that right from the get-go, my college experience was centered on one person only: Bob.

• • •

Having made first chair of the Illinois All-State Orchestra in high school, I thought I was pretty well prepared for college orchestra—so I was definitely *not* prepared for the comedown of being assigned last chair during freshman year. The University of Illinois attracted a lot of very good musicians, many of whom had studied in conservatories, and I quickly found myself on the bottom looking up. For as well as I played violin, there was still a lot I didn't know about music theory and the finer nuances of playing.

I struggled in my other classes, too, which were a lot more difficult than I'd expected them to be. It's not easy for Black students to make the transition to college, particularly at big public universities where we're usually just a tiny sliver of the student population. When I started at the University of Illinois, I was one of only a few hundred Black students at the entire school—just about 1 percent of the student body. I was the only Black undergraduate in the school of music. And yes, I continued to hear the same kind of ignorant and racist comments from students as I'd heard from that girl in the All-State Orchestra. In the 1960s, you couldn't be the lone Black face in a historically white space without hearing the comments and feeling the side-eye.

Once again, my salvation came in the form of teachers who mentored me. At Susan's urging, both Dan Perrino and Paul Rolland took me under their wings. Dan was a whirlwind, a dynamic force on campus who created and nurtured ensembles such as the Black Chorus and the Afro-American Cultural Program (even though he was white). He was like everyone's favorite uncle, always looking for ways to create music, and no matter what problem popped up in my academic or personal life, he was always there, ready to help.

Paul was my violin teacher, a native of Hungary who created

his own system for teaching string instruments. When he immigrated to this country in the late 1930s, he noticed that American students played violin with stiff and robotic motions, causing tension throughout their bodies. Paul believed they should learn to play with more balance, better posture, and a more fluid motion, and he applied for a government grant to study the problem more thoroughly. In 1966, the year I started college, he launched the University of Illinois String Research Project, and he hired me to work on it. He must have liked how I played, because he ended up using me in a series of educational films about proper technique—some of which are still in use today.

Just as I had with Susan, I felt like Dan and Paul "got" me in ways my peers didn't. That said, I did enjoy spending time with Bob and his fraternity brothers, many of whom were smart, funny, and ambitious young men. One of Bob's best friends, Preston Pearson, would go on to become a professional football player for the Dallas Cowboys and Pittsburgh Steelers, and another, Virgil Hemphill, would end up working with us at Black Entertainment Television. I liked hanging out with the guys at the Kappa Alpha Psi house, where Bob was one of the more popular brothers—even after he got kicked out of the frat for hazing a pledge.

I wouldn't have fit in there without Bob, as I'm sure the guys thought I was square as all get-out. I didn't drink, smoke, or do any kind of drugs. I spent my time in the library or in the music school, or at my part-time job at the YMCA. A lot of the girls who hung out at the fraternity house were real partiers, or they belonged to their own little sorority cliques. But while a few of the sororities wanted me to rush, I turned them all down. Even the Chi Omega house—a white sorority—came calling, probably wanting to be able to claim a Black girl in their ranks. But I just wasn't a joiner. And beyond that, I had a lingering feeling that even if I became a member of a sorority, I still wouldn't really fit in.

I felt the same way about the Black Power movement, which was then on the rise across US college campuses. As Black students began embracing their heritage, growing out their Afros, wearing dashikis, and having sit-ins, I felt the paleness of my skin more than ever. Maybe the activist students would have accepted me in their ranks, I don't know. I never felt comfortable enough to try. I still felt like an outsider everywhere except in the orchestra—same as I had in high school.

The truth is, I still sometimes feel like an outsider, even today. I still wonder why friendships with peers seem to come more easily to others than they do to me. Perhaps it's a natural result of all that moving around when I was a child, of never having a chance to create deeper bonds before pulling up stakes and leaving. Or maybe I just am a "different egg," a person who doesn't quite see the world as others see it. Sometimes I think it has to do with a quote attributed to Denzel Washington: "Some people will never like you, because your spirit irritates their demons." So, maybe my spirit is fine, but it happens to hit others in a way that makes them feel uncomfortable. Of all the possibilities, I suppose I'd like to think that one is closest to the truth. But the reality is, I will probably never know.

Bob graduated in the spring of 1968, at the end of my sophomore year. He had decided to pursue becoming a diplomat, so he applied to and got into the Woodrow Wilson School at Princeton University, which was trying to attract more non-white students to its program.

He moved to New Jersey to start graduate school, and very soon he was running up big phone bills, calling me in Illinois every night to talk—and to check in on me. Bob wanted to know where I was and who I was with, and he didn't like it if he called and I didn't pick up the phone.

I missed Bob, but now that he was eight hundred miles away, I was focused on other things. A few of the guys I knew were urging me to try out to be a cheerleader, because there weren't any Black people on the squad. "Come on, Sheila," one of them said, "get in there and teach them how to dance a little bit!" Now that Bob was gone, I had more time on my hands, and I'd always liked cheering in high school—in part because in those pre–Title IX days, it was one of the rare "sports" available to women. I decided to go for it, and at the beginning of my junior year, I became the first Black cheerleader at the University of Illinois.

Being a cheerleader was like doing gymnastics workouts, and it exercised a different part of my brain than my music studies. It was also just a lot of fun. We'd cheer at all the pep rallies and football games, and we also got to take part in other high-profile campus activities, such as "tapping" the homecoming court.

By tradition, the cheerleading squad would go with the school mascot, Chief Illiniwek, to dorms and Greek houses to let people know they'd been nominated for homecoming queen or king. One night in the fall of 1969, we gathered outside the Alpha Kappa Alpha house and shouted for Charlynn Chamberlin to come out. She was a gorgeous young woman with a towering Afro, one of three Black students (out of ten total) nominated that year. She came hurrying out of the house with a big smile on her face, then ran straight over to hug me, the only Black girl on the cheerleading squad. Unfortunately, the candle I was holding got too close to her hair, and before we knew what had happened, half her Afro was on fire! She dropped to the ground and started rolling around, and thank goodness she wasn't hurt. Charlynn went on to become the first Black homecoming queen at the University of Illinois, and I'm just glad I didn't accidentally kill her before that could happen.

To my mind, cheerleading was mostly just an enjoyable way to keep in shape. But the music school administration took it as a sign that I wasn't serious enough about my studies—even though I had been steadily moving up in the orchestra and was now doing very well in all my classes. I was informed that because I'd joined the cheerleading squad, I would be kicked out of the music school and stripped of my scholarship. This decision was not only ridiculous, it was unfair and most likely racially motivated, because I can't imagine the university kicking a white cheerleader out of her major. The administration even made some comment that I might hurt my fingers while cheerleading, as if that were a valid reason to completely derail my studies.

I was dumbfounded at the fact that the department was coming down on me so hard. But instead of quitting cheerleading, I called Dan Perrino and told him what was happening. "Oh no," he said. "I am not sitting still for this one." He went straight to the dean and pleaded my case, and he got the decision reversed—yet another example of a mentor lifting me up in a moment when my life was threatening to go completely off course.

So I was able to keep on cheerleading, and I had a really fun time doing it. I started getting some attention from other guys and even went on a few dates. I figured that since Bob was at Princeton, and I was still just nineteen years old, I might as well spread my wings a little bit. But Bob was absolutely not having that. Only a few weeks into my junior year, he took a leave of absence from his Princeton program and came hurrying back to Illinois.

Now, there are several ways you can look at that decision. Some people might see it as a romantic gesture—a man coming back to be with the woman he loves. Some might see it as resulting from a combination of factors; maybe Bob was struggling with his classes, or feeling lonely, or missing not just me but his fraternity brothers too. Maybe Bob wasn't quite ready to grow up yet, and this was his way of extending his college experience.

There's another way to look at it. Maybe Bob was a jealous man, and he did not want me dating anyone else. But instead of talking with me about it, maybe coming to some sort of understanding about what would happen during the two years we would spend apart, he straight-up walked away from his Ivy League graduate program and came back to "claim" me. He needed to control the situation, and this was how he knew he could do it.

I don't say this lightly. I say it because of what happened just after he got back to Champaign. We were at the Kappa Alpha Psi house, talking about our relationship and the dates I'd been on with other guys, and Bob just kept getting more and more worked up. "Let me tell you something, Sheila," he said, staring at me intently. "You are going to be *with me*." I started to say something back, and in a flash, Bob threw his fist into the wall behind me, punching a hole into it.

I was stunned, and honestly, a little bit scared. He hadn't swung at me, but the violence of the act shocked me. Yet I also felt something else. *Look at how much he cares about me!* I thought. Since the day my father had walked out, I had felt unloved, never good enough. But here was proof that I was worth fighting for. My dad might have been as cold as ice, but Bob loved me with a red-hot intensity that he couldn't control. I should have been alarmed by what he had done. Instead, I felt flattered.

One person who did feel alarmed by Bob's behavior was Susan Starrett. I had started confiding in her about my relationship with him, and she saw the red flags that I was busy staring right past. She came to see me in Champaign one afternoon, and Bob happened to drop by the music school while she was there. I introduced them, and he left after a short conversation, but that was enough for Susan to make a more clear-eyed assessment of him than I would for many years to come. "Are you sure he's the quality of person you want?" she asked me. Was she asking me whether he was the type of man I wanted? Or whether he was good enough for me? I wasn't sure. But either way, I believed the answer was yes.

Bob took a job in Champaign with Project 500, a program aimed at bringing more minority students to the university. In the fall of 1967, only 372 out of 30,400 students were Black—just over 1 percent. The following year, Project 500 would bring in 565 new Black and Latino students. The university wasn't really prepared, and some of the new minority students got stuck in subpar housing, resulting in protests and mass arrests at the Illini Union. But ultimately, the program would be a success, leading the way to a more fully integrated student body.

For us personally, Project 500 meant that Bob had a decent-paying job that would allow him to stay in Champaign while I was still in school. He had decided he wasn't leaving without me, which soon led to his next decision: that it was time for us to get married.

I don't remember how Bob proposed, or where we were, or anything about it, really. I'm pretty sure he just announced that we needed to go ahead and do it, then handed me a ring. It's possible that he made more of a romantic gesture and I've just blocked it out. Either way, the fact that I have no memory of that moment speaks volumes.

We got married midway through my junior year, in January 1969. The ceremony and reception were very modest, because we had almost no money. I had taken up sewing after my dad left as a way to bring in a little extra money, and by this time I was quite good at it, so with the help of another girl in my dorm, I sewed my own wedding dress. Paul Rolland very kindly arranged a string quartet to play for us. And because I was a cheerleader, we were allowed to use the campus chapel for free.

It was a small wedding, just some fellow students, our families, and a few other friends. Susan Starrett came, although she had recently become more vocal in expressing her concerns about Bob. She knew about the record album he'd given to another girl, and about his jealous fits, and she didn't believe that he was going to be faithful to me. Susan even went so far as to say, "Sheila, please don't marry him. I'm telling you right now, I don't think it will end well." But I wouldn't listen. I loved him, and I believed he loved me, because he kept telling me he did. And if he had some qualities I didn't like, well, maybe over time I could change him. When she saw that I had made up my mind, she changed her message. She just looked me in the eye and said, "If you ever want to get out of this, I am here to support you."

My mother also didn't want me to marry Bob. I didn't know it at the time, but she actually called Tom Purce that week. "Sheila is getting married," she told him, "and you need to get out here and stop it." I suppose she thought he'd fly right out and sweep me off my feet and away from Bob Johnson forever. But that didn't happen. I don't know how Tom responded to her, but he was busy having his own college experiences, and I'm sure he had a girlfriend of his own at that point.

Even if he had flown out, it wouldn't have mattered. I was twenty years old, an adult now. I was in love with Bob and determined to make this marriage work. So determined, in fact, that I ignored the biggest, most shocking red flag of all, which came up on our wedding night.

When the ceremony was over, Bob and I went to a nearby motel to spend our first night together as a married couple. We had only just checked in when he said, "I've got something to do"—and then he left.

I sat down on the bed, wondering where he'd gone and when he'd be back. It was weird that he'd just walked out like that, but maybe he was planning something nice? Was he going out for flowers or to bring us a bottle of champagne? I waited for a while. And then I waited some more. And then the sun went down. And I was alone, in a motel, on my wedding night.

And that's when I realized he wasn't coming back.

Which is exactly what happened. Bob walked out *on our wedding night*, and he never returned. This was long before anybody had a cell phone, so there was no way to reach him. Not that he would have responded if I had tried.

As I sat there on that bed, shame spread through me like hot poison under my skin. How could this be? How could this man, who had told me so many times that he loved me, who had put a fist through the wall at the thought of losing me, abandon me on our wedding night? Was he with another woman? Had he gone out to a bar? I didn't know and couldn't bear to think about it. Because the only thing that really mattered was that he'd chosen not to be here with me.

I began to cry, the big heaving sobs of someone who knows she's made a terrible mistake but can't see a way to take it back. My mother had collapsed on the kitchen floor after my father walked out, and I had vowed in that moment that I would never, ever put myself in that position. Now, just four years later, here I was, abandoned by my husband just as my mother had been abandoned by hers.

I called my mother, and she drove right over. She was beyond furious. "You are not staying in this marriage," she told me, her eyes wide and nostrils flaring with anger.

"Mom," I said, my voice breaking, "I love him. I can't leave him."

Now she was furious with me. "Sheila, you are making a big mistake," she said. "Look at what he's doing! You cannot stay with him!"

But even in the depths of my misery that night, even knowing that Bob had humiliated me beyond all reason, I was determined to stay with him. To make it work. To change him. Why was I so determined? Maybe I couldn't admit that I'd been wrong about him. Maybe I was still terrified by what had happened to my mother that night in our kitchen in Maywood. Somehow, it felt more important to hold on to my new husband than to admit what was happening. It felt more important to save my marriage than to respect myself. If I had to live in denial to keep my relationship going, then that was what I would do.

They say that when something goes wrong in a man's life, he'll blame others. But when something goes wrong in a woman's life, she'll blame herself. I blamed myself for Bob's behavior. I internalized the idea that I had displeased him or I wasn't good enough. And so I made up my mind to be better. I had to persevere, to win him back.

I did this because I believed that, deep down, he loved me. I had to believe that, because the alternative was too painful and frightening to contemplate. And I would spend the next three decades trying to hold on to that belief, in spite of so much evidence to the contrary.

By this time, the Vietnam conflict was raging, and now that Bob wasn't a student anymore, he was no longer protected from the draft. Sure enough, his number came up, and he was drafted into army service.

I was shocked. We had only just gotten married, and now my new husband was going to be shipped to Southeast Asia, to fight a war in the jungles there? Upset, I called Dan Perrino and told him what was going on. "He should try to get into the reserves," Dan advised me. According to him, the reserves had to have a certain percentage of minorities within their ranks, so Bob would have a good chance of getting in and remaining stateside.

Bob did get assigned to the reserves, and the army instructed him to report to Fort Leonard Wood, Missouri, for basic training. He reported in the fall of 1969, just as I was starting my senior year of college, and did eight weeks of training there. And then he returned to Illinois, where he would be required to serve only on weekends unless he was called up for active duty.

I was glad to have him back, relieved that for the time being, at least, he was safe from having to fight in Vietnam. We were living together in an apartment now, and I decided to make our home as nice as possible for the upcoming holidays. I bought us some Christmas decorations and a tree, and made sure we had all the foods he liked and a pile of gifts for him to open. This would be our first Christmas as a married couple, and I wanted it to feel special.

And then the letters started coming. They were from a woman in Missouri, addressed to Robert Johnson. Who was she, and why was she writing to my husband? I asked Bob what was going on, and he just looked at me. Then he chuckled. "Oh, those letters aren't for me," he said. "There was another guy with that same name in my unit. She must have gotten us mixed up." This made no sense, of course. Even if there was another Robert Johnson in his unit, how would the woman have gotten our address?

"Are you sure?" I asked him.

"Oh, yeah," he said. "They're for that other Bob Johnson." Then he told me to give him whatever letters came in, saying he'd make sure they got to the right guy. "I'll take care of it," he said with an absolutely straight face.

Again, I chose to believe him. Because the alternative felt worse.

I had one more semester of school left, but now that Bob was back from basic training, he decided he'd had enough of Illinois. "I need to get back to my program," he told me. "Come on, let's go ahead to Princeton. I've stuck around here long enough."

For once, I told him no. "Bob," I said, "I'm on scholarship! I'm not going anywhere until I graduate." I knew that if I left the university early to follow Bob to the East Coast, I'd never get my degree. Reluctantly, he agreed to stay until I finished. Because I had dared to push back and even deny him what he wanted, he clapped back with one more move to reestablish control.

"Then we'll leave as soon as you finish your last exam," he said. "There's no sense waiting around for graduation. We need to get where we're going." The commencement ceremony was scheduled for a couple of weeks after that, so professors could get final grades in. Of course I wanted to attend my college graduation—and my mother wanted to as well. But Bob was absolutely adamant. "I came back here for you!" he said. "I sacrificed two years. You can sacrifice that."

And so I did. As soon as I finished my exams, we packed up our car and lit out of Illinois. My mother cried when I told her. She was upset for me, but his behavior also rubbed like sandpaper on the places where she was still raw from my father's leaving. I couldn't bear to make her so unhappy, and I couldn't understand why Bob was incapable of letting me enjoy the graduation day I had earned. But he was my husband, and I wanted *him* to be happy. So, off we went to Princeton, to begin our new life together.

Four

MUSIC, MUSIC, MUSIC

B ob and I had almost no money between us, so when we moved into our one-bedroom apartment in Princeton, I got to work trying to figure out how to make it look nice without going broke. We were staying in a grad-student dorm, a modest little space on the eighth floor of a high-rise. I called a furniture warehouse in High Point, North Carolina, and ordered some black leather couches, a chair, and a table for our living room. At about $400, this was the biggest purchase we had made as a married couple, and we had to set up a payment plan.

Even though Bob had a scholarship, it didn't pay for groceries, gas, car insurance, or any of our other daily living expenses, so I had to start working right away to make sure our bills got paid. With the help of the University of Illinois's job-placement office, I got hired as the middle school music teacher for the Woodbridge Township School District. There were five middle schools in the system, which meant I'd be teaching at a different one each day of the week.

Throughout the 1970–71 school year, I spent hours driving up and down Route 1, hustling to keep five different orchestras on track.

In the spring of 1971, Bob landed a summer internship working with NATO in Brussels. He was hoping to become a Foreign Service officer, and getting the chance to work with the new political head of the US Mission to NATO, Lawrence Eagleburger, was a dream job. As soon as school was out, I flew to Brussels, too, excited to spend a couple of months in Europe.

Like many Foreign Service spouses, I underwent "training" for how to become a diplomat's wife. I took classes in etiquette and presentation, learning which spoons to set out when having an ambassador over for dinner. I also took a wine-tasting class, which marked my first time ever drinking alcohol. I liked it fine but still didn't drink a whole lot while I was over there. Most of my time was spent practicing my violin, listening to the radio (we didn't have a TV), and exploring Brussels. And at the end of Bob's internship, we spent a glorious few weeks traveling through Europe, riding around in a big black NATO car that was too big to fit through half those narrow streets.

We had a great time that summer, but when we got back to Princeton, we had only about $50 left in the bank. I knew I could feed us for a week on $25 worth of groceries, especially if I clipped some coupons out of the newspaper. I was a big coupon clipper in those days, always trying to figure out how to get more with less, like it was a game.

Tired of driving up and down Route 1, I managed to get a job teaching orchestra at Princeton Day School for the 1971–72 school year. PDS, as it's called, was (and still is) one of the best schools in the country, and the kids who go there get a great education. But I have to admit, I also got an education there—of a very different sort.

This was the early 1970s, which was a whole new era in terms of sex, drugs, and whatever else people wanted to get into. As I soon discovered, there were a lot of weird things going on at PDS that the administration probably knew nothing about—spouse swapping, key parties, married people suddenly deciding they swung both ways. Some professors openly smoked pot, even inviting students to take part, I guess as a mind-expanding exercise. I was still as square as could be, so for me, all the carrying on among PDS faculty and parents felt like having a front-row seat to a strange and seamy soap opera.

I just kept my head down and kept teaching, grateful to have a job I enjoyed that paid the bills. But halfway through the first semester, I decided to spread my wings in my own little way when the PJ & B Players (named for Princeton Junction & Back, the little two-car train that ran between town and the Amtrak station) put out a casting call for *Fiddler on the Roof.*

Not only had I never acted, I obviously didn't fit the usual demographic for this beloved Jewish musical. But the producers cast their net wide, bringing in more than 140 performers for the production. And they didn't seem to mind that I wasn't an actor, casting me for the role of Fruma Sarah, the butcher's dead wife. The part was crazy fun—I got to claw my way out of my grave and screech-sing at Tevye for letting his daughter marry my widowed husband.

How could you let your daughter take my place? Live in my house,
carry my keys and wear my clothes, pearls, how?
    Pearls!
    Pearls!
    PEARLS!!

I was so excited to be in the musical, even though it ran for only five performances. If the McCarter Theatre hadn't been booked immediately after with another show, we would have done more, as our *Fiddler on the Roof* had the biggest advance sales in the history of PJ & B (at $2.50–4.50 a ticket, a bargain even then). The play was just a lark for me, a fun thing to do after my workday at PDS. But it would help me get a role in another production just two years later, which would lead to one of the biggest—and luckiest—coincidences of my life, decades down the road.

By the time Bob finished his master's degree in the spring of 1972, he had decided the Foreign Service wasn't for him. Instead, he took a government-appointed job at the Corporation for Public Broadcasting, a nonprofit created by President Johnson to support public television. Within a year, he would also take a job with the National Urban League, a civil advocacy organization. This marked the start of his interest in Black social power and TV—a combination that would later become the basis of Black Entertainment Television.

We packed up all our things, including those black leather couches (which we would hold on to for a good long while), and moved to Washington, DC. We rented a two-bedroom apartment at 2121 P Street NW, just a couple of blocks west of Dupont Circle. After living in grad-student housing, we thought our new place felt enormous, with a spacious living room, a long hallway, and two bathrooms. I decorated everything in black and white, to go with our living room furniture, and we began to explore life in the nation's capital.

The first job I got was as a research analyst on Capitol Hill, but I really wanted to get back to teaching. I contacted Sidwell Friends, another of the top-rated K–12 schools in the country, and pitched them on creating an orchestra program. They had a choir teacher but no one teaching strings, so I went in to try to convince them that I was the person to do it. Headmaster Bob Smith seemed interested, but he had one question for me: "Can you play guitar?" I couldn't, but I wasn't about to tell him that. "Of course!" I lied. And I got the job.

Plenty of rich and well-connected families sent their kids to Sidwell, but there was no money in the budget for a strings program. So we started holding fundraisers to pay for music and music stands. Luckily for me, a lot of parents were excited at the prospect of having an orchestra, so people eagerly jumped in to help raise the money we needed. A huge percentage of the middle school kids signed up for string lessons, and pretty soon we had a thriving program.

I didn't know it at the time, but the seeds of this orchestra would blossom into Young Strings in Action, a groundbreaking musical group that I would lead for many years to come, even after leaving Sidwell. We called it Young Strings in Action because our players didn't just sit like robots on chairs—they got up and danced. The kids got to bop all around the stage while they played, and they just loved it. YSA became my signature group, and I'd eventually take them on the road for tours, up and down the East Coast and beyond.

That was all in the future, though. For now, I was just trying to get the Sidwell orchestra off the ground, working my butt off for the grand salary of $7,200 a year. I know that doesn't sound like much in today's terms, but let me tell you: it wasn't much then either. And that's especially true considering the entitlement that wafted off some of these students.

There was one girl in my string class who just could not stop acting out. She wouldn't listen and was constantly cutting up. I tried to be patient, but she finally got on my last nerve. "You have got to sit down and listen," I told her. "That is just *enough*." I thought that calling her out might shame her into behaving, but I was wrong about that. Because she straight-up called me the N-word, in front of the whole class.

My blood ran hot. I just could not believe that word had actually come out of her mouth. "You're coming with me," I said, and I marched her down to the headmaster's office. Bob Smith was mortified, of course, and he immediately called the girl's father, who was a donor to the school and a wealthy businessman. And that's when all hell broke loose. The father pushed back, suggesting that I was at fault for having provoked his darling daughter. He actually said I should be fired, which left me even more shocked than the girl's outburst had. I looked at Bob Smith and said, "If you fire me, I will have Jesse Jackson, Al Sharpton, and everybody else up here." But I didn't need to worry about Bob—he had my back right from the start. He was as horrified as I was, and he quickly shut down any suggestion that I would lose my job.

Sometimes I wondered whether that would have been a blessing, though. Because as much as I loved teaching the kids at Sidwell (well, most of them, anyway), I just couldn't keep doing it on such a low salary. The truth of that was brought home to me in 1973, when I discovered I could make a lot more money doing something else I loved: acting.

I had heard about auditions for a Washington Theater Club production of a new play, Lonne Elder's *Ceremonies in Dark Old Men*. This was a touring show, with most of the roles filled by actors from the

New York–based Negro Ensemble Company, so there wasn't much available for local actors. But when one of the actresses had to drop out just a week before opening night, the director rushed to hold auditions. I went out for the part—and to my surprise, I got it.

The role was small but juicy: I'd be playing a hooker named Candy who uses her feminine wiles to trick a mob boss into giving up his recipe for bootleg whiskey. I had to dance around the stage singing "Sweet Georgia Brown" while trying to get him drunk. When I finally got him into bed, cooing at him to give me the recipe, he suddenly started snoring. It was a fun part to play, and the audience cracked up every time.

The *Washington Evening Star* newspaper thought it was so hilarious that a middle school music teacher was playing a prostitute, they did a story about me:

Nighttime finds Sheila Johnson prancing the stage, in her professional debut, as a naïve, sassy chick in "Ceremonies in Dark Old Men."

During the day Sheila worries about "Winnie the Pooh," the next musicale of her fifth-grade class at Sidwell Friends School . . .

"The kids, the faculty are so excited it's unbelievable. Especially the kids because now they can say not only does she teach violin but she's an actress," gloats Sheila, a bubble-faced and curvaceous 24-year old.

I'm not sure how "bubble-faced" I was, but I did have a good time slinking around and cursing up a storm as Candy, even though it scandalized some of my students. One of them told me, "Mrs. Johnson, I can't go to see the play because it's rated X." The show got fantastic reviews, and we ran for ninety-eight performances, one of the longest-running productions in Washington in the early seventies.

Because my time onstage was short, I spent a lot of time in the "greenroom" offstage. I'd bring my violin and practice fingerings, or read a book, but only rarely mingled with the other actors in the play. A lot of them knew each other from New York, and they just had a different vibe going on. They'd pop out into the alleyway beside the theater and smoke pot, and although they sometimes invited me, I always said no. I still had never tried drugs, and besides that, the alleyway was trash strewn and smelly. Not that the greenroom smelled much better, thanks to the dead rats in the walls. DC in the seventies was a pretty rough place.

There was one other actor who didn't really hang out with the New Yorkers—the other local performer in the production, a guy named Bill Newman. Bill was playing the part of Theo, one of the bootleggers, and I soon discovered that not only was he a brilliant actor, he was a sweet and thoughtful man. He and I would talk in between scenes, and unlike the New Yorkers, he didn't tease me about being so square. We had come from similar backgrounds, as he'd grown up in a middle-class family in Arlington, Virginia. He'd been trying to make it as an actor in New York but had recently returned to the DC area.

Bill and I became friendly, though we never saw each other outside the theater. I loved talking to him, but I was married and it would have been strange to try to see him socially. But there was one time when I invited the whole cast over to our apartment for a party, and he came then. I had prepared a nice spread of hors d'oeuvres and cocktails, and many years later, Bill would tell me that he was impressed when he walked in the door. I suppose he was surprised that a couple in their early twenties had their own two-bedroom apartment and were having a party with actual glassware and snacks that weren't made by Frito-Lay.

When our run of ninety-eight performances was over, I got the whole cast to sign my playbill. Bill wrote, "Sheila—The foxiest lady in DC. It has been fantastic working with you. Let's stay in touch. Best wishes always, Bill Newman."

We didn't stay in touch, though. In fact, I didn't see Bill again for three decades. But I wouldn't forget those hours we spent together in that greenroom, enjoying each other's company and chatting away the time.

Even though I was onstage for just twenty minutes each night, I made almost $30,000 for my performance in *Ceremonies in Dark Old Men*—more than triple what I made for a full year's work at Sidwell. And I knew exactly what I wanted to do with that money. At age twenty-four, I was ready to buy a house.

I was reading the *Washington Post* over breakfast one morning when I saw an ad for new town houses in Southwest DC. There was nothing in that part of the city in those days—no restaurants, few stores, nothing really to draw anyone there. Though the Southwest waterfront today is a bustling and happening part of the city, in the 1970s it was a run-down, economically dead area. These new town houses cost less than $20,000 each, and you just had to put down $5,000, so I persuaded Bob that we should buy one. He had just taken a job on Capitol Hill, which was only a short commute from Southwest, so he agreed.

Bob had become the press secretary for Walter Fauntroy, DC's first congressional representative. Walter was on his way up at that time, a pastor and civil rights activist who had been close to Martin Luther King Jr. and helped plan the March on Washington. Although his seat in Congress was nonvoting (because DC isn't a state), he became influential on the Hill anyway, cofounding the Congressional Black Caucus and introducing legislation that would benefit DC residents. Walter was a fixture among the Black elite of the city, and also a fellow Kappa Alpha Psi, so Bob felt like he'd made it to the big leagues.

That might have been true, but we were definitely not living like it in our strange little part of DC. Our P Street neighborhood had been colorful, with drug users and gay men populating the block. There was a gay bar called the Fireplace a couple of doors down from our building, and a grassy area called P Street Beach where men would go to hook up. But I had liked living there—it felt safer than Southwest DC, which at that time had a darker, more dangerous feeling.

Street crime was a way of life down in Southwest, and Bob and I were constantly dealing with break-ins to our house and car. We got tired of walking outside to find the car's windows smashed, and more than once somebody popped the hood and stole the battery. There was just a feeling of desperation, and even at our local Safeway store, gangs would be hanging around in the parking lot. One afternoon when I drove down there to get groceries, I was shocked to see a young girl hiking up her dress to show herself off to the men in the parking lot, and I just couldn't take it anymore. I drove away without even getting my groceries, and I never went to that Safeway again.

For the most part, Bob and I got along in those early days. He was happy working in Representative Fauntroy's office, getting to rub shoulders with important people in the worlds of politics and media. He was often out in the evenings, coming home very late at night, and I wasn't always sure what exactly he was doing. Despite our wedding-night fiasco, which I was trying very hard to forget, I was still pretty naïve—a Miss Goody Two-shoes who just assumed that her husband had work obligations and that was that. I would commute to and from my work at Sidwell, take care of the house, and make sure the refrigerator was always full. And I also started giving private lessons to a few students, which I soon discovered paid much better than my teaching position.

Around this time, Bob started picking at me about little things. Once, when he brought a colleague home, I fixed dinner and brought their plates to the table. Bob took one bite of his, looked at me, and announced, "This food is terrible. I'm giving it to Old Yella." Was he joking? I wasn't sure. "Well, who's Old Yella?" I asked. In response, he stood up, carried his plate into the kitchen, and scraped his food into the trash can, which happened to be yellow. I just stared at him, while his friend squirmed at the table.

Now, I might not have been Julia Child, but I knew I could cook. So I didn't take that particular criticism to heart. Maybe Bob was just trying to show off? It didn't make sense, as his words had made his friend even more uncomfortable than they'd made me. I just resolved not to cook that particular dish again and tried to forget about it. Which I obviously failed to do, as I still remember it fifty years later.

I wanted to please Bob. I wanted him to feel like I was a good wife. And I suppose I thought that by purchasing the town house, bringing in extra money, and keeping him fed and comfortable in a nice home, I might earn his approval. But it seemed like the more I tried to please him, the more he tried to knock me off balance.

"You know, people don't really like you," he'd say. "You think you're *all that*, but you're not." He seemed to enjoy lobbing little insults my way. Some of them, such as criticism of my looks or my figure, hit me in tender spots and made me feel terrible. Others, such as criticism of how I taught music, didn't. I knew I was a good teacher, because people—students, parents, Susan Starrett, Paul Rolland—constantly told me so. But nobody was around to tell me that I wasn't ugly or that people actually liked me. So, those comments began to sink in, and I began to wonder if they might actually be true.

Every now and then, my old boyfriend Tom Purce (who now went by his middle name, Les) would come through Washington. He was elected to the Pocatello city council in 1973 and would go on to become the first Black mayor of the city, so he started making trips to DC for political conferences and meetings. He'd stop by to visit, or maybe just to check to make sure I was doing okay. He was always so solicitous and kind, so easy to be with and complimentary. And at the time, he wasn't married, so I'd have these little inklings of thoughts in the back of my head: *Oh my god. Why am I not with this man?* I wondered if I had made a big mistake, but it felt too late even to consider. I was married, and I was loyal to my husband.

Who, by the way, didn't seem to appreciate Tom's attentiveness to me. One night after Tom had come for dinner, Bob offered to drive him back to his hotel. I don't know what was said in the car, but I didn't hear from Tom again for years.

· · ·

In just the second year of my time at Sidwell, the orchestra was already flourishing. I decided to take them on tour, raising money through concerts and fundraisers, and the parents really stepped up. We held a dinner concert in the cafeteria, with the orchestra playing and a group of dads cooking the meal. Once we raised enough money for the bus and hotels, I took the orchestra up to Princeton, to play in my old stomping grounds. The kids loved it, feeling like real professionals as we played for receptive audiences in new venues.

Yet even as supportive as the headmaster and school had been, I knew it was time for me to leave Sidwell. As soon as I'd started teaching students at home, I realized I could make far more money as a private instructor than I could as a schoolteacher. But I wanted to do more than just teach students individually. I wanted to take the seeds of what I had created at Sidwell and form an independent orchestra. I asked a number of the parents if they'd be willing to support Young Strings in Action even if it was no longer affiliated with Sidwell, and they all said yes.

So the first part of my plan was in place. Now there was one more important step to take, and I'd be on the way to creating my own full-time music business.

I had already begun giving private lessons while still at Sidwell, but I never felt comfortable asking students to drive all the way to our funky neighborhood of Southwest DC. Instead, I'd face the traffic myself, driving all over town so I could teach them at their own homes. We needed to upgrade to a better house in a better neighborhood, so students could come to me. But the good news was, I had been right about the wisdom of buying in Southwest: just two years after buying our town house for a little under $20,000, I was able to flip it for three times that much. With the money we made, we were able to buy a beautiful home for $115,000 on Brandywine Street NW, in an upper-middle-class neighborhood just west of Rock Creek Park.

Once we had the Brandywine house, I began hustling to grow my business. I took on as many students as I could and started building Young Strings in Action into a powerhouse orchestra. I kept track of every single penny that went in and out, writing off every expense that I possibly could. Because I was running my business out of the house, we wrote off one-third of the mortgage. Every paper clip, every roll of toilet paper, every violin string, we wrote off. I studied the tax laws like I was cramming for the LSAT. And in just two years, I went from making $7,200 to making $68,000 a year. I also got tax money back from the government, because I had done my homework and kept such good books.

Funnily enough, some students—or their parents, anyway—became suspicious about how we managed to do so well. One of my best students, an Indian American violinist, was mortified when her father expressed shock that Bob and I, as a Black couple, could have such a nice home. He told his daughter to poke around and find out whether we were actually in the "drug business." I just couldn't believe it; there's no doubt whatsoever that he would never have asked such a thing if Bob and I were white. And it wasn't as if this girl's parents didn't like us. They were always very friendly to my face. But this was the kind of racism that persisted.

While teaching was my passion, I discovered during this period that I also had a strong entrepreneurial streak. I knew that not many people were able to make a living in music, and I didn't want to be stuck in a low-paying job in order to do what I loved. I needed to find a way to make money in music, and so I did. I also handled all the finances for Bob and me, built up our savings, and made sure we were able to afford what we wanted during this time.

I kept up a few other side hustles too. Paul Rolland had been writing music textbooks for Boosey & Hawkes, one of the largest publishers of classical music in the world. But when he suddenly suffered a heart attack, the company asked me to step in to finish his work, which included volumes on teaching private lessons and orchestras. I got paid to finish Paul's books, then received residuals from their sales. And I continued working on the University of Illinois String Research Project, which eventually sent me to Europe to teach. I taught at Homerton College, at the University of Cambridge in England, and also started taking my Young Strings in Action orchestra overseas, to places like Salzburg and Gstaad.

I was incredibly proud of making a living in the arts, as I could see that other musicians whom I'd studied with were struggling. This was a wonderful time in my life, both creatively and professionally. I thought back to that moment when I stood onstage as a thirteen-year-old, hearing the roar of the audience after I finished playing Bohm's "Perpetual Motion" and vowing to myself that I would make a living in music. And now I was doing it.

Sometimes, when I was on the road in Europe, I'd call home to tell Bob about a performance or an experience with the kids. Because I was in time zones that were either five or six hours ahead, it was hard to reach him in the evenings in DC, as it was the middle of the night where I was. So I took to getting up early in the morning and calling him then. The problem was, no matter how late it was in DC, he often didn't pick up. Midnight, one a.m., two a.m. . . . I'd call, and the phone would ring until our answering machine came on. There were still no cell phones then, so there was no other way to reach him.

Where was he? I didn't know, and I didn't ask. Because I didn't really *want* to know. It just felt easier that way.

Meanwhile, Bob had just taken a job lobbying with the National Cable Television Association, and our lives were about to change—dramatically—once again.

Five

MAKING A BET

One evening in 1976, Bob went to a party at the house next door to ours on Brandywine. He was being his usual extroverted self, chatting up everybody within earshot, and he ended up in conversation with a woman who worked at the National Cable Television Association. NCTA was a political lobbying group that represented the cable industry, which was then in its earliest days. Although HBO had been launched a couple of years earlier, cornerstone networks like CNN, ESPN, and TBS were still in the future, so this really was a brand-new industry.

Hearing Bob smooth-talk his way through the party, the woman apparently thought he'd make a good lobbyist, so she suggested he give NCTA a call. He was intrigued, in part because he'd already started talking with Representative Fauntroy about how they might use fledgling cable networks to get information out to constituents. Bob believed there was a big future upside in cable, and his experiences at the Corporation for Public Broadcasting, at the National

Urban League, and on Capitol Hill made him a perfect candidate for NCTA. Soon enough, he landed himself a job there.

Bob was hired as a vice president, and he got to work lobbying for cable TV companies. The next two years were like an education on steroids: he got to know the entrepreneurs who were starting and running cable networks, learned about the technology, and spent hours talking about the regulations, budgets, and strategies for these companies. All these conversations lit a fire in him. He had spent his career so far working in nonprofits and government, but now he was getting a taste of the thrill of starting a business. He began to think about how he might get in on that action himself.

One of NCTA's board members was an entrepreneur named John Malone, who headed a company called Tele-Communications Inc., or TCI. Bob talked with him often, and at one point John told him he was looking for cheap programming to fill time on his Memphis cable network. Memphis had a big Black population—more than 40 percent and growing—and John needed programming that would appeal to that audience. Bob took it a step further. He asked John whether he thought there was a market for an entire network aimed at the Black demographic. Now John's eyes were the ones lighting up. He asked Bob to draw up a proposal.

When Bob got home that night and told me about the conversation, he was practically buzzing with excitement. But researching and writing that kind of document wasn't an easy task—and when was he going to find time to do it? One day not long after that conversation, Bob brought home a full proposal and dropped it on our dining room table. It wasn't for a Black network, though—it was for a network for viewers over the age of fifty.

Bob had gotten this document from a guy named Ken Silverman, the founder of a cable company called Cinemerica. Ken had come to DC to get NCTA's help lobbying for a planned seniors network, to be called Cinemerica Satellite Network. On reading his proposal, though, Bob was less interested in helping Ken than he was in "borrowing" his work. He asked him if he could use the proposal as a blueprint for creating his own Black cable network, and Ken said, "Sure." So Bob brought it home, plopped it on our table, and got to work whiting out all the references to "the elderly" or "seniors," replacing them with the word "Black," and updating the rest of the document to reflect our demographic.

Just like that, we now had a solid proposal and an expressed interest from John Malone. Now we just had to find some seed money to get "Black Entertainment Television" off the ground.

In May 1979, Bob flew to Las Vegas for the annual NCTA convention. He started telling people about his plan, and in the course of the three-day event he found himself talking to a guy named Bob Rosencrans, who headed UA-Columbia Cablevision. Like John Malone—in fact, like most of the cable operators in those early days—Rosencrans was looking for programming to fill unused blocks of time on his network. He offered Bob two hours of airtime every Friday night, if Bob could come up with good programming. To do this on his own, Bob would have had to spend hundreds of thousands of dollars for a transponder, studio, and facility expenses. But Rosencrans offered him the opportunity for free, because getting this new demographic of Black viewers would benefit him too.

That two hours a week of programming was all we needed to take the next step. Bob quit his job at NCTA that summer, then wrote up a press release announcing the creation of Black Entertainment

Television. I signed for a $15,000 loan, and Bob also managed to negotiate a $15,000 consulting gig with NCTA. With that $30,000 nut, we were ready to start our own cable business.

On September 13, 1979, we paid $42 to the DC government to incorporate BET. We started the company with one hundred shares, worth $10 each, for a valuation of $1,000. We split the shares among the three members of our first board of directors: Bob, me, and our lawyer Joe Sharlitt. If either Bob Rosencrans or Ken Silverman had asked for a little piece of equity in exchange for the building blocks they'd given us, we probably would have done it, especially since we had nothing else to give them. But neither one of them asked for anything, a decision that Rosencrans would later call "the biggest mistake of my life."

Now that BET was incorporated, it was time for Bob to pay another visit to John Malone. In November 1979, he flew to Denver, where TCI was based, and talked to him about our plans for the network. To Bob's surprise, John didn't need to be persuaded at all. "How much do you need?" he asked. John was a smart investor, and he already understood that BET was a home-run idea.

John proposed to buy 20 percent of BET for $180,000, then provide $320,000 more over time in the form of loans. A half million dollars, just like that! At incorporation, we had set the value of the company at a thousand dollars, but with a stroke of his pen, John Malone wrote a check that valued our company at $900,000. John and Bob signed a letter of agreement on November 12, 1979, stipulating that Bob would have full operating control of BET, while TCI would get a board seat. And that was that. Except for one thing.

As Bob was walking out the door, he turned to John and said, "Hey, I've never run a business. Do you have any advice?"

John just looked at him and said, "Get your revenues up. Keep your costs down." Simple as that.

Bob flew back to DC ready to spend some of that money. Our launch date was set for January 25, 1980, so there was no time to waste—we had to find office space, hire a staff, figure out programming, and perform a thousand other tasks. Even though my hands were full with my music business, I jumped right in, spending hours working together with Bob to get our new cable company launched.

We found a three-room office for rent in the old American Trial Lawyers Association building in Georgetown, then started filling it with office equipment. Chairs, desks, telephones, filing cabinets—we had to buy absolutely everything, right down to the Post-it notes and paper clips. We also hired three people as BET's first staff, all of them women whom Bob knew. Two of them had worked with him at NCTA, and the third was his sister.

Vivian Goodier, who went by the nickname "Chickie," was our first hire, as vice president of affiliate relations. Then Bob's NCTA secretary Carol Coody came over to work as his special assistant. Bob's sister Paulette came on as comptroller, relocating to DC from Waukegan, Illinois. Bob had nine sisters and brothers, but he was closest to Polly, as she was called. And she had some experience doing accounting, so he felt comfortable entrusting her with handling our little company's finances. Among the three of them, Chickie got the highest salary, at $40,000 a year. Polly agreed to work for $25,000, and Carol would be paid $14,000. In the beginning, Bob didn't take a salary, as we needed every penny of John Malone's investment just to get off the ground.

Even with that $180,000 initial investment, though, it was soon obvious to both of us that we wouldn't have enough cash to make it to launch. There were just so many startup expenses, from paying the deposit on our office space to hiring lawyers for the reams of paperwork that needed to be filed. Every time we turned around, there was another invoice that needed to be paid, and the money was flowing out too quickly. But where could we get another financial infusion, fast? We didn't want to sell more of the company, and we weren't in a position to get any kind of loan. We desperately needed some fast cash, or the company might collapse before it ever got going.

One evening, after spending a few hours crunching the numbers and fretting, the answer came to me. "Bob," I said. "I can sell the Landolfi."

He just looked at me. He knew how much I loved my violin, and we both knew how much my parents had sacrificed to get it for me. That violin represented my mother's dreams for me and her belief in my abilities. It was truly a special instrument, like an extension of my own arm. But it was the only item we owned that could instantly bring in the kind of cash we needed to make it to launch.

Bob didn't try to talk me out of it. He knew we needed the money. We had big dreams, and to make them come true, I knew we would have to make sacrifices. So the next day, I took my Landolfi to Weaver's Violin Shop in the Maryland suburbs and sold it for $26,000—which would turn out to be just enough to get us to the launch. And I bought another, much cheaper violin, so I could keep teaching and playing to pay our bills at home.

I didn't tell my mother right away, because I was afraid of her reaction. But after a few weeks went by, I felt worse keeping it a secret from her. When I told her, she flared with anger. "Do you know what I went through to get that violin for you?" she demanded.

"Mom, I know," I said. "And I'm sorry. But I had to do it for the company." I understood why she was upset, but I was playing a long game. If this BET idea worked the way Bob and I thought it would, I'd be able to buy any violin I wanted down the line. I truly believed that. And I demonstrated that belief every time I signed my name to loan paperwork or put in unpaid hours building the business—or sold the most precious object I had ever owned. I was determined to do whatever I needed to make this work.

As our launch date drew near, Bob hustled to line up ad sponsors. We decided that our first broadcast, for two hours on the evening of January 25, 1980, would be of a 1974 movie called *Visit to a Chief's Son*. The movie was about a white anthropologist and his son who visit Kenya, then learn life lessons from a Black father and son in the Maasai tribe. It wasn't very subtle, and the movie wasn't exactly a blockbuster, but I guess we thought it would be an appropriate way to kick off the world's first Black-oriented cable network.

We decided to throw a launch party, but because Washington, DC, wasn't yet wired for cable, we had to hold it in Northern Virginia—otherwise, we wouldn't have been able to see our own network. Even though Bob had managed to get advertisers such as Pepsi and Kellogg's on board, that money wasn't rolling in yet, so we were still pretty broke. We served potato chips, sodas, and beer and wine to about ten people in a room at the USA Network. The whole thing felt a little bit like a college party, at least until Bob stood up to speak.

As modest as this beginning was, Bob started talking in grandiose terms about where Black Entertainment Television was heading.

He quoted William S. Paley, the founder of CBS and one of the most visionary early TV pioneers. One of Bob's old fraternity brothers, Virgil Hemphill, had flown in from Chicago for the launch, and he couldn't help but chuckle watching Bob go on and on like some kind of mogul. BET was hardly anything yet, but to hear Bob talk, we were going to take over the world.

I believed, as Bob did, that we were onto something potentially very big. But that night, I was just relieved we had made it to the launch. I ate a few potato chips, had a glass of wine, and couldn't wait to get home to catch up on some much-needed sleep.

At first, BET had only two hours a week of programming to fill. Easy enough—we could just air a movie every Friday night, and that would be that. But this was not a sustainable business, so we needed to start getting more hours right away. And the only way to do that was to travel around to different markets, asking cable providers to sign us.

Bob started traveling all over the country, sitting down with mostly white executives to explain to them why they really needed to carry Black Entertainment Television. As you might imagine, this wasn't an easy sell in 1980. What really surprised us, though, was that even when we started signing deals and having our programming in different markets, we still struggled to get advertising, even from Black companies. Bob had managed to get a few advertisers on board for our launch, but he had a hard time convincing other companies that Black TV programming was a good place to spend their advertising dollars. This felt like a deeply entrenched racism, where no one—not even Black-owned companies—could believe BET might produce the returns that a white cable company would.

But Bob didn't give up. I give him credit where credit is due: he worked his butt off, traveling around to cable companies and advertisers, swearing to them up, down, and sideways that BET was the real deal. He and I would talk about the company's latest moves and deals when he got home, but I was still working more than forty hours a week on my various music businesses. I had to, because Bob still wasn't earning much of anything at BET. I kept all our books at home, and the bulk of our income was coming through my music ventures. It just wasn't possible for me to switch to working full-time at BET—we couldn't afford it.

Even so, I spent as much time as I could at the Georgetown office, pitching in and just trying to keep an eye on what was going on down there. Working at a startup is stressful, and everyone was overloaded. Polly and Chickie seemed to argue half the time, and Bob grew frustrated with his sister, who wasn't as polished as he was in dealing with people. Some days, you could hear the yelling all the way down in the garage. Bob was about to tear his hair out, so as soon as we had enough advertising dollars coming in, he called Virgil Hemphill and asked him to come work at BET. Virgil took a leave from his teaching job in Chicago and came straight to DC.

We started programming more hours—six per week now—and expanded beyond movies into sports. Sports broadcasting was big business in America, but even though ESPN had launched in September 1979, it didn't show games played by Black colleges and universities. To fill the gap, we started programming football and basketball games from schools like Grambling and Howard. Bob would travel to the games, often with Chickie Goodier, and interview the college presidents at halftime. He liked being on camera, and the interviews were a good way to get information out about these Black schools. And then we discovered another big cultural gap that needed filling, in music.

In August 1981, a new cable company called MTV launched, and suddenly everybody was on fire to watch music videos. But MTV's executives refused to play most Black artists' videos, supposedly because their music wasn't "rock 'n' roll." David Bowie even called the network out in an interview with VJ Mark Goodman, asking why MTV wasn't featuring Black artists. Goodman actually said, "We have to try and do what we think not only New York and Los Angeles will appreciate, but also Poughkeepsie, or pick some town in the Midwest that will be scared to death by Prince—which we're playing—or a string of other Black faces."

This was straight-up racist crap, obviously—bad for the country but good for BET. As soon as we could get the programming, we started playing all the videos by Black artists that people were hungry to see. We started a half-hour program called *Video Soul*, which was cheap to make and brought in thousands more viewers. Virgil Hemphill put on a shiny suit and called himself "Reverend Eldorado," hosting the show until we hired a young DJ named Donnie Simpson to host an expanded version of it.

By 1982, our programming and staff were growing fast. We hired a young woman named Janis Thomas as VP of advertising services and a guy named Jeff Lee to work on programming. Bob negotiated a deal with Taft Broadcasting Company to sell another 20 percent of the company for $1 million, which gave us a valuation of $5 million. In October 1984, we began programming twenty-four hours a day.

Less than four years after launching, we had eighteen million subscribers and more than three dozen employees.

As the business grew, we moved to bigger offices in the heart of Georgetown, on Prospect Street. With a staff made up mostly of young, talented, ambitious African Americans, the feel inside the building was electric. There was something special going on at BET, and people were excited to be part of a Black-owned business that was growing so fast.

Bob made himself the face of the company, and that was fine with me. I was proud of what we were doing but didn't feel the need to be in front of any cameras or parading myself around the office. He liked being the center of attention, and the way I saw it, if he succeeded as CEO, we both would be successful. In fact, I became his biggest advocate, constantly talking up his brilliance and applauding the moves he made. I felt like that was my role, but sometimes it actually seemed to irritate Bob. "You act like you're my cheerleader," he would say. "You've got to stop doing that."

I never was sure why it bothered him so much, but looking back, I wonder if he was feeling guilty. Because while I was busy singing his praises and working around the clock to keep our home and our company running smoothly, he was—of course—running around on me with one of his employees. I didn't know it at the time, but I would find out a few years down the road in a soap-opera-worthy turn of events. I loved Bob, and I wanted so badly for us to succeed. But the harder I worked and the more I sang his praises, the more irritable he became.

Yet even though I was his cheerleader, I wasn't afraid to push back if I thought he was going down the wrong path for the company. One Sunday evening, Bob and I were going around and around about some decision he'd made, and I got so pissed off that he wasn't listening to me, I picked up the phone and called Jeff Lee at home. Poor Jeff had been relaxing in his living room watching *60 Minutes*, but as soon as he made the mistake of picking up, I launched into a detailed explanation of what Bob and I had been arguing about.

"Jeff, you need to tell Bob to *listen to me*," I said. All Jeff could think was, *Oh man, Bob is my boss*. He tried to be diplomatic and walk straight down the middle, saying, "Bob, she's got a point. But you make a good point too . . ." It's funny now, but at the time, Jeff was sweating.

The bigger BET grew, the more I was learning about how to run a business. I tried to keep an eye on what our employees were doing and how much money was coming in and out. I also did our books at home, managing our household and keeping track of various revenue streams.

And that's when I noticed that something very strange was going on.

"Bob," I said one evening in the summer of 1985, "why does your paycheck keep changing?"

"What are you talking about?" he asked. Now that BET was on steadier financial ground, Bob was taking a salary, but I had noticed that the amount on his paycheck was different every single time. Why would it go up and down? Shouldn't he be receiving the same amount each payroll period?

"I don't know, and I don't care," he told me. "They know what they're doing over there. Don't worry about it."

I tried to put it out of my head, but this just seemed fishy. And then I noticed something else strange: Polly had bought herself a Mercedes and had begun wearing designer clothes to the office. I wasn't the only one who had noticed, either. People had begun whispering about it, wondering how, on those early low salaries, Polly was suddenly swanning around like a Hollywood starlet.

Bob confronted Polly, who cussed and swore to high heaven that she hadn't stolen anything. "How *dare* you accuse me?" she shouted at him. But all the signs pointed in that direction—and if she was siphoning money out of his salary, that would explain why his paycheck kept going up and down.

We shut down the office for a couple of days and brought a private investigator in to get to the bottom of the situation. Sure enough, Polly appeared to have left a trail of stolen money. It looked as though she had not only embezzled money out of people's paychecks, she also had been using her company credit card to buy clothes and other items for herself. Bob was furious with his sister, but he didn't have the heart to fire her. After getting her to sign a note promising to repay the money she'd taken, Bob decided to look the other way. But someone else in the company wasn't so forgiving.

In mid-July, John Malone received an unsigned letter from someone at BET. It was full of details of Polly's alleged embezzling:

> I regret that I am the one who must inform you of the unlawful
> act of embezzlement that has been carried out by one of Black
> Entertainment Television's highest-ranking employees.
>
> It has come to my attention that Miss Paulette Johnson,
> vice president for finance and sister to the president of the com-
> pany, has embezzled funds from BET thru the use of her as-
> signed company American Express card. Ms. Johnson has used

her card for the purchase of personal items to the tune of over $28,000 between the period of October 1983 and April 1985 without any attempt to reimburse the company prior to being caught. Ms. Johnson was "caught" and her charges verified with the American Express Company thru an outside auditor. She was not terminated. Instead, she was given the proverbial "tap on the wrist." This incident is being kept quiet only because she is the president's "sister." Anyone else would have been terminated immediately or prosecuted.

John Malone wasn't the kind of man who was easily shaken. He just jotted down the words "Ask Bob for explanation," handed the note to his secretary, and waited to hear what Bob would say.

Bob didn't want to fire Polly, but in the end there didn't seem to be any other choice. He told her not to come back to work, but Polly wouldn't hear of it. "You can't fire me," she told him. Instead, she informed him that she was quitting, and that she wanted compensation for unused vacation days and a severance package. According to Polly, Bob's response was, "Bitch, you will get nothing from me until you crawl."

The clash between Bob and Polly went instantly from zero to a hundred, and I just tried to stay out of it. But Polly started calling the house, begging me to intervene, screaming about how badly Bob was treating her, and even telling me she was going to kill herself. "I can't help you," I told her. I knew Bob could be harsh—he had been terrible to me enough times for that to be absolutely clear. But she was as bad as he was, as far as I was concerned. I just couldn't believe a sister would steal from her brother's company. It was so brazen, so disloyal.

Then again, Bob had the kind of leadership style that seemed naturally to lead to a lot of interoffice turmoil. Carol Coody left just a month after Polly did. And Chickie Goodier had already gone, back in 1982, after some kind of disruptive dynamic had developed between her and Bob. I didn't know what that was about. But as I would eventually learn, everyone else in the office sure did. As with so many of Bob's offenses, I would be the last to find out.

Six

FAMILY

One afternoon in December 1983, I was conducting my Young Strings in Action orchestra at the Old Post Office, the gorgeous Classical Revival building near the White House that would later become the Trump International Hotel. Right in the middle of a concerto, I heard a scuffling and murmuring in the crowd behind me. I didn't know what was happening, but we just kept going, and when we finished the piece, the packed audience burst into loud applause.

I was gesturing to the kids to stand up and take a bow when a man walked up to my podium.

"Could you keep the orchestra onstage?" he asked.

"I'm sorry," I said, flustered at the man's sudden appearance, "but what's happening?"

"Her Majesty wishes to meet them," he replied with a slight bow.

"Whose majesty?" Now I really was confused.

"Queen Noor of Jordan," he said, and broke into a smile.

Aha, so *that's* what the murmuring had been about. As we were playing, the queen of Jordan and her entourage had glided into the room, turning everybody's heads. When I got my first glimpse of her, I understood why people had started whispering. Queen Noor, a Syrian American named Lisa Halaby who had married King Hussein five years earlier, was absolutely radiant. She had blond, shoulder-length hair, blue eyes, and luminous skin, and she carried herself in the most regal way. She was the most magnificent-looking woman I had ever seen in person.

She walked up to the stage and extended her hand. It was an honor to meet a queen, but even though she carried herself like royalty, she had actually been born right there in Washington, DC, and gone to school in New York. Yet she spoke with what sounded like a slight British accent when she said, "Mrs. Johnson, the performance was wonderful."

I turned to the orchestra and introduced her to them as "someone important who would like to meet you." The kids had no idea who she was, of course, but hearing the word "queen" got them excited. And then Queen Noor thrilled them even more by going from student to student, shaking each one's hand and complimenting their playing. When she got to our five-year-old violinist, Johnisha Matthews, the girl's eyes got as big as saucers. She was a sweet, talented little kindergartner, and she and the queen seemed equally captivated by each other as they chatted onstage.

The man who had first approached the podium came up to me again once the queen had finished shaking all the kids' hands. "Your orchestra is fantastic," he said. "So diverse and talented. Are you free tomorrow night at eight o'clock to come to the home of the Jordanian ambassador?"

"I would love to," I said. "Is this for an event?"

"Just come," he said, again flashing that big smile. "We will explain everything then. We will call you tomorrow with details of how to get to the residence."

Well, this was mysterious. I had no idea what to expect, but the following evening I made my way to the home of the ambassador of Jordan—or, as it's formally called, the Hashemite Kingdom of Jordan. The Jordanians had also invited Esther Coopersmith, a board member of the Capital Children's Museum, which was one of Young Strings in Action's sponsors. Esther was a real mover and shaker in Washington, a former representative to the United Nations, and she loved YSA. She got a big smile on her face when she saw me; I suspect she knew why we had been invited.

I was escorted into a lavishly decorated living room, where I took a seat on an overstuffed sofa. A couple of men started asking me questions, at first about the orchestra, but then about my political views. For some reason, they asked me if I knew Jesse Jackson, and I said that I'd met him several times. They asked me about a few other people, and just as I was wondering what this was all about, a few more men walked into the room. They sat on chairs facing me, and one of them began fiddling with beads on a string. I don't know why that detail has stuck in my mind all these years, but I just remember watching him move the beads around with one hand, constantly in motion as he asked me more questions.

"Her Majesty would like to invite your orchestra to the Jerash Festival," one of them finally said. They showed me a video promoting the annual event, which Queen Noor had started two years earlier and which mostly featured Jordanian artists. "We have never had a children's group perform there, but we would be honored to have your orchestra as our guests."

It's difficult to convey just how much this meant to me. For ten years, I had been working to make YSA the premier strings group for young people in the mid-Atlantic region. After leaving Sidwell in 1974, I had hustled my butt off to teach as many students as I could, to pull together the best of the best, and to turn them into a creative, accomplished orchestra. We had kids from ages five to eighteen, all of whom were not only talented musicians but great performers and dancers too. Whenever we got up onstage, everyone got so into the music, we brought down the house every time. This orchestra was my heart, and the success and growth of these students was my proudest achievement so far in life. And now, all that hard work was paying off with an opportunity beyond all our wildest imaginings.

We had traveled up and down the East Coast, getting rave reviews everywhere we went. But this was on a whole different level: we would be guests of King Hussein and Queen Noor, playing at the ruins of the Temple of Artemis in the ancient city of Jerash. I was so excited for the kids, I could barely speak. But I managed to squeak out the words, "We would be honored"—and then doors swung open and several women burst into the room carrying big platters of lamb, rice, hummus, and stuffed grape leaves. It was time to feast, and this was only the beginning of what the Jordanians had in store for us.

The festival was scheduled for August 1984, so we had some time to plan. Our full orchestra had more than one hundred members, but we'd have to whittle that down to sixteen, plus one piano accompanist, for the trip, as the king would be flying us over on one of his private planes.

I started talking to some of the parents, gauging their interest and the students' availability. A few of the Jewish parents were worried about sending their kids to an Arab country—and of course, if they had been to Israel and had that stamp in their passports, that could present a problem getting into Jordan. So we began working with the State Department to try to get waivers for those students. Some other parents were concerned about what kind of food would be available on the trip. We'd be visiting with Jordanian families, and I guess they were worried that the local cuisine wouldn't be palatable to their children. I thought, *You have got to be kidding me! This is the chance of a lifetime, and you're worried your son might not like falafel?*

There were dozens of groups scheduled to perform, but most were from Jordan, and only three were from the United States. So we decided to go full-on American for the program. We hired a costumer and designed Western-style outfits for everyone, in red, white, and blue material and with little cowboy hats for the boys and sashes for the girls. I chose classical pieces by Vivaldi, Bach, and Telemann but also decided to throw in some traditional American songs, like the nineteenth-century fiddle tune "Turkey in the Straw."

As the date of the festival drew near, the kids got more and more excited. I did, too, though it was hard to leave BET in its fledgling stage, with all that tension roiling between Polly and Bob, and the network struggling to find its way to a profit. But though I was spending as many hours as I could at BET, my music career was still paying our bills at home—and besides, I wouldn't have missed this opportunity for anything. Jordan felt like a magical, faraway place of legend, and I couldn't wait to see it.

Jerash is sometimes called the "Pompeii of the East," as it has the most extensive, best-preserved Roman ruins outside of Italy. And the

Jerash Festival was held in the shadow of the most spectacular ruin, the two-thousand-year-old Temple of Artemis.

During the grand opening ceremony, all the invited groups paraded down the cobblestone Sacred Way, toward a grand amphitheater. As I walked along that ancient path, the views of the ruins and the hills beyond just took my breath away. It was like strolling into history—but although some of the bands played while walking in, I was terrified our smaller kids might trip on those cobblestones, breaking a wrist or sending their violin flying. The Dixieland Jazz Band was in front of us, and as they blared out a joyous tune, our whole group danced and bopped up the walkway. It was all so festive and fun, and the kids were loving every moment.

King Hussein and Queen Noor were seated in the amphitheater, and as we drew close, they stood and walked over to greet us. And not only them—their armed security guards came over, too, holding big rifles that freaked a couple of the kids out. But the king and queen hugged each student, welcoming them personally.

The concert was the next day, and when our moment came, we really turned it on. As the only children performing in the festival, our kids got more than their share of attention. And when eight-year-old Burleigh Seaver and ten-year-old Antonia Fasanelli stepped up for solos, the crowd went absolutely nuts. By the end, the audience was cheering, clapping, stomping, and throwing flowers up to the stage. The whole experience was just magical.

We stayed about two weeks in Jordan, playing a couple more performances but also getting a chance to tour the country, including sightseeing in Amman, visiting the ruins of Petra, and floating in the Dead Sea. The kids were amazed—they had no idea that they would be received so warmly and have such a great experience. One, Nora

Maccoby, later told a reporter that she had "expected to find a strange place, with burning hot weather and full of weapons, but we have come to a lovely country full of friendly people." They even got paid, something like $50 each, which made them feel like real professionals.

For me, this was what music was all about: making connections among people. Seeing the faces of these children light up, knowing that they were experiencing potentially life-changing moments—all of this served to clarify why I had chosen music as a career.

It also clarified something else, something that had been burning like a small ember inside me but was now growing hotter and more urgent with each day. Seeing those children, sharing these experiences with them, served to remind me how badly I wanted to have children of my own.

Bob and I had been trying for a while to get pregnant, but it just wasn't happening. By the time I went to Jerash, I was thirty-five years old, and Bob and I had been married for fifteen years—so if we were going to have kids, we needed to get on with the project. But I knew that if I hadn't gotten pregnant yet, my chances weren't going to improve as I started coasting toward forty.

It drove me crazy that I couldn't get pregnant. I was healthy, Bob was healthy—I just didn't understand what the problem was. Bad thoughts started to creep in, that I wasn't good enough or that somehow this was all my fault. I already spent so much of my time trying to make sure that I didn't let Bob down about other things. And now here I was, letting him down about the biggest, most important thing of all. These feelings kept gnawing at me, until finally I decided it was time to go in another direction.

"Bob," I asked him one evening, "can we try adoption?"

He looked at me for a moment, then said, "Why?"

I mean, I thought it was pretty obvious, but if he needed an answer, I had one. "Because I *really* want a child," I told him.

And to my relief, he simply said, "Okay."

I had learned about an organization called the Barker Adoption Foundation, a nonprofit based in Bethesda, Maryland, that helped place babies into loving families. We started the process with them, and with each step we took, I could see Bob warming up to the idea. In 1985, we were able to bring home a newborn girl, whom we named Paige. I can still remember the feeling of holding her in my arms for the first time; it was the most joyous moment of my life. She was such a precious little girl, my own little doll baby, and I loved everything about her—the way she smelled, the way she looked at me when we cuddled, her soulful eyes. I thought she was the most beautiful child I'd ever seen.

Bob and I were over the moon, ecstatic to have this baby girl in our lives. He really connected with her, and for the first time in, well, maybe ever, I saw a sweeter side of him emerge. I could feel him bonding with this child, and that gave me hope. I had felt a rift growing between my husband and me for a long time, but like so many women, I felt that maybe having a baby would bring us closer. For a few months, it seemed like that might actually happen. But like so many of the hopes I clung to in our relationship, this one would eventually be dashed too.

In the meantime, I got even more deeply involved with bringing music to Jordan. Queen Noor had been so delighted by our orchestra that she invited us to come perform several more times. And she also asked me to help establish a conservatory for young musicians in

Amman. I couldn't bear to be away from Paige, so I would bring her with me when I traveled there. I invited an old friend, Alice Queen, to accompany us and help me take care of her. In the early 1970s, Alice had been the nurse at Sidwell and one of the only other Black people on staff there. She and I had bonded back then, and I was happy to have her come along for our adventures in Jordan.

And they truly were adventures. Young Strings in Action ended up playing in Jordan four more times over the next four years. We not only played again in Jerash, we also had the honor of playing for heads of state and for Mrs. Anwar Sadat. I got to know Queen Noor pretty well, and one day in 1988, she got all excited about the fact that Sean Connery was shooting an Indiana Jones movie in Petra. She decided to fly down to watch the filming, but at the last minute, word came down from King Hussein that she better turn around and get herself back to Amman. The king wasn't about to have his gorgeous wife flying off to meet with the lady-killer Sean Connery.

As we started working on the conservatory, I flew to Jordan every three months or so, to help set it up and teach the Young Strings method to Jordanian music instructors. When the queen first asked me to help, I had thought, *Yes! This will be a cakewalk!*, figuring that the Jordanian government had all kinds of money to fund it. Instead, she told me we needed to raise the funding for it—so I got to work on that too. I arranged a big evening at the Four Seasons Hotel in Georgetown and invited the great Pearl Bailey to emcee and sing. Mayor Marion Barry and Representative Fauntroy cohosted the event, and of course our orchestra played. But the highlight of the evening came when Pearl Bailey picked up her microphone, threw it aside, and said, "I don't need this. I was in show business before they had electricity!" She belted out "Hello, Dolly!" and people couldn't get their checkbooks open fast enough.

The National Music Conservatory opened in Amman the following year, 1986, and dozens of Jordanian kids signed up. By 1987, the conservatory had upward of seventy young people studying violin, and plans were in the works to expand instruction into brass and woodwinds. In fact, thirty-five years later, the conservatory is still going strong. I'm so proud of bringing music instruction to young people in Amman, and I truly loved the years I spent traveling there.

The only time I can remember feeling a little strange was one night in 1988, the last time we brought Young Strings in Action to Jordan. On the night of our big concert, as I walked up to the podium to conduct, I could hear a collective gasp from the audience. This conservative Arab crowd was absolutely shocked, and probably a little scandalized, that a woman in my condition would travel all the way from the United States. And my "condition" at that point was as plain as day.

I was, incredibly enough, pregnant.

After all those years of failing to conceive, and having stopped trying once I became a mama to my beautiful Paige, I began to notice some strange changes in my body as I approached forty. I occasionally felt bloated and nauseated, and I seemed to be gaining weight, but I couldn't figure out why. I finally went to see a doctor, who ran some tests, broke into a smile, and said, "You're pregnant."

I was absolutely stunned, and maybe afraid to believe it was really true. I had wanted this for so long, and had been so disappointed when I couldn't get pregnant, that it felt scary to celebrate. But when

I told Bob that night, he didn't have any of those kinds of complicated emotions. He just seemed proud and happy.

Bob was kinder and more considerate of me during my pregnancy than he'd ever been. He bought me racks full of maternity clothes, and for the first time in our marriage, he began telling me how beautiful I looked. It was as if my being pregnant validated him, and he couldn't wait to show me off to the world. This was a really nice time for us, and my pregnancy went along without complications, which was a relief. I got bigger and bigger and felt the baby start kicking. Paige couldn't wait to have a sibling, and I couldn't wait to give her one.

I carried the baby into the ninth month, and then one morning when I was at Paige's preschool in Cleveland Park, I felt the first pangs of labor. But even though I had never given birth, I felt like these weren't normal labor pains. I can't really describe the sensation, other than to say that something just felt very off. I hurried to the hospital, then called Bob's office. Michelle, his secretary, told me he was on his way somewhere and she couldn't reach him. "Tell him he needs to get to the hospital," I said. "As soon as he possibly can."

The medical staff whisked me away, and after doing tests and ultrasounds, one of the doctors came to my bedside with a grim look on his face. "There's a complication," he said. The baby's internal organs were in the wrong place—they had moved into his chest cavity, crowding his lungs. This was due to a condition called diaphragmatic hernia, where the muscle between the abdomen and chest cavity doesn't develop properly. Our baby boy, whom we planned to name Geron, was struggling already, even still in the womb. But when he came out, he might not be able to breathe at all.

I couldn't believe what I was hearing. My heart began pounding, and I started to cry. As of that morning, I'd had no idea anything was wrong with the precious baby inside me, this child I had been carrying for nine months. And now these doctors were saying that I had to have an emergency C-section right away, because Geron was not likely to live—and if I didn't have the procedure immediately, it was possible that I would die too.

Bob arrived at some point during all this commotion, but I barely noticed, as the medical team had prepped me with anesthesia and painkillers and who knows what else. I was an absolute mess, groggy and crying, but I felt the doctors pull my son out of my body. He looked perfect, but instead of wailing like a healthy newborn, his voice was silent. But he struggled and fought for breath like the brave little boy he was.

Geron was born alive, and he lived for one hour on this earth. And then he took his last, labored breath and died in my arms.

One hour. That's how long we had together. I can't even put into words how cruel and agonizing it felt to watch my baby's life slip away. I don't believe words exist that can describe the pain of losing a child in this way. I was in shock, looking at Geron's sweet face, kissing his cheek, wetting his tiny body with my tears. I would have done anything to will my boy back to life. But he was gone.

Bob was right there, and he was crying too. In all our years together, I had never seen him cry—and I never would again. "He looks like me," he said, choking out the words. He held the baby, too, but eventually, a nurse came and gently took Geron away.

I don't remember much else about that day, as I was lost in a haze of pain and grief. But I do remember that Jeff Lee came by, as we had become close in the time that he was working at BET. He offered me words of solace, the kind of things you say when you don't know what to say. And as he bent down by my bedside, I whispered, "Jeff, he lived for a little while." He hugged me, and the tears came again.

Walter Fauntroy came to the hospital too. In that moment, he wasn't a congressman, or Bob's former boss, or a civil rights activist. He was a pastor, there to offer comfort in my time of need. But I'm not a religious person, and I wasn't sure about the solace he seemed to be offering. As he prayed over me, I said, "Walter, why do such terrible things happen to good people?" I couldn't imagine why a just God would crush a person with such an overwhelming burden of grief.

"Sheila," he said, "this is God's way of preparing you for whatever's going to happen next. It's building your strength."

We buried Geron in a tiny white casket, laying him to rest at Fort Lincoln Cemetery in Brentwood, Maryland. Bob took care of all the funeral arrangements, as I was incapable of doing much of anything. Though he never gave any indication that he blamed me for the fact that Geron died, I absolutely blamed myself. "Bob," I said through my tears, "I'm so sorry I failed you." I felt like he had done his part— he had gotten me pregnant, and I was the one responsible for carrying and giving birth to a healthy baby. And I had screwed it up.

I know that doesn't make sense, but where Bob was concerned, I had gotten to the point of feeling like I couldn't do anything right. From our very first months together, he had established a pattern of acting out, then making me feel like a fool when I asked him about it. When I asked about my missing record album in my freshman year, he came back with "What are you talking about? You must have misplaced it." When I asked about the letters from the woman in Missouri, he dismissed my worries with a lie about some other Bob

Johnson. Whenever I'd ask him why he was coming home so late or why he didn't pick up the phone at two a.m., he acted like I was crazy for wondering.

This was classic gaslighting, and he did it *all the time*. He wasn't the kind of person who'd say, "Look, Sheila, I'm a man and I'm just going to do what I want to do." That would have been painful, but at least it would have been honest. Instead, he would say, "Maybe you need to get some help, because you're imagining all this." I wasn't strong enough to say, "Hell no, I'm not"—because I wasn't sure. I loved him. I trusted him. Probably, unfortunately, even more than I trusted myself. I ignored my own gut instincts for years, because I didn't want them to be correct.

And yet . . . every so often, Bob gave glimpses of some inner decency—enough that they kept me in the marriage, kept me hoping that our union would settle down into something more stable and that felt more secure. When I watched him splash around with Paige at the beach, or weep at the loss of our baby, I could see that he had a softer side to him. That was the Bob I wanted, the man who could be sensitive, kind, and caring. But that Bob was fleeting. And although our children could bring it out in him, he exhibited none of those qualities with me.

A few weeks after losing Geron, I took Paige on some errands. She was just four years old then, and although we had explained to her what had happened, I wondered how much she truly understood. When we got to the bank that afternoon, I found out.

Paige walked into the bank with me, holding my hand. As I got in line for our regular teller, she decided to make an announcement.

"Listen, everybody!" she said in her reedy little voice. "My mommy was pregnant, but she's not anymore. We lost the baby, so don't say anything."

A couple of people glanced my way, some with sad looks in their eyes, and I just stood there, dumbfounded. This was the sweetest gesture, revealing an empathy and understanding beyond my daughter's years. Nobody thinks about this, but when you give birth to a baby that doesn't survive, *everybody* asks you about it. They've seen your belly get bigger and bigger over the months, they've made comments and gotten excited with you as you got closer to your delivery date. And when they see you're no longer pregnant, they naturally assume you have a baby now. When you give birth to a child who dies, you can't just hope no one notices. You have to explain it to literally everyone, not only friends and family and colleagues, but also bank tellers and store clerks and accountants and anyone else who saw you radiantly, happily pregnant.

Unless you have an extraordinary, thoughtful child who steps up to do it for you.

Three months after losing Geron, Bob and I adopted a beautiful boy we named Brett. I would never really get over the loss of Geron, but having my precious Brett and Paige made our family life complete.

As 1989 drew to a close, my life changed in other significant ways too. BET had finally reached profitability, but the culture at the network was suffering. We were heavily in debt from all the loans we'd taken as a startup, and the quality of programming was going downhill, with raunchy music videos and infomercials for household gadgets making up too much of our schedule.

This was a critical time at the company, and John Malone had planted the idea in Bob's head that we should start considering an initial public offering of stock—an IPO. "I need you at BET," Bob told me one night. "Full-time."

I had been teaching music for seventeen years and had achieved every goal I'd set for myself in that arena. I had introduced hundreds of children to the joys of string instruments and orchestral music, and many had gone on to play professionally. The conservatory in Amman was going strong, and the Jordanian government had even given me its highest award in education—an honor that was only slightly tarnished by the fact that Bob refused to come to Amman for the ceremony. (I took my mother instead.)

As much as I loved teaching music, it was time for BET to take precedence. As the 1980s drew to a close, I came on board as the executive vice president of corporate affairs. BET had survived its first decade. Now we needed to take it to the next level.

Seven

GOING PUBLIC

One afternoon back in 1985, a young woman with bright eyes, caramel skin, and a scarf wrapped around her head came walking into BET. She was a skinny little thing, shy and polite. But when she opened her mouth to sing . . . *oh my god*. Whitney Houston had the voice of an angel, and she had come to BET to promote her new single, "You Give Good Love."

I got to meet Whitney that day, and I was struck by her innate sweetness, her open face and polite manner. I loved her music, too, which was melodic and showed off her five-octave vocal range. Her debut album, which had just come out, was full of hits—instant classics like "How Will I Know," "Greatest Love of All," and "Saving All My Love for You." And her videos were as wholesome as those songs, each of them telling a story and focusing on her singing and musicianship.

Four years later, when I came to BET full-time, music videos weren't like that anymore. I had loved them from the first ones I saw, as they seemed like a new art of storytelling. The fact that MTV was slow to play Black artists' videos offered us a great opportunity to showcase Black talent and give our viewers something they couldn't get anywhere else. Those early music videos really hit a chord with BET's audience, and they enabled us to sell a lot of advertising for our original programming, like Donnie Simpson's *Video Soul*, that covered them.

But very quickly, the videos turned from musical storytelling into something else. They started getting raunchy, focusing on sex and money and objectifying young women. I couldn't believe some of the images that were coming across our network—if you turned the sound down, it looked like pornography. I had two young children now, and half the time I couldn't even have BET on at home, because I didn't want them seeing those images. And the percentage of time that BET was showing videos just kept going up and up, so much that by the mid-1990s, they would make up more than half of our programming.

Maybe I was being a prude, but I wasn't the only one bothered by the turn these videos had taken. Tom Joyner, who became one of the most popular Black radio hosts in America, would later tell the *Forbes* magazine writer Brett Pulley that BET had "gotten to the point where you don't want to come home and turn it on . . . If you have your pastor over, you are sure not going to turn it on. And if you have white friends over, you're not going to say, 'Hey, you need to check out BET.' I've been inside Bob's office, and he doesn't even have it on in there."

Bob didn't care. He was focused on doing whatever it took to get the money pouring in, and music videos were a cheap way to get viewers. Whenever I suggested to him that we had a responsibility to the Black community to put out higher-quality content, he'd just roll his eyes and say, "It's Black *Entertainment* Television. That's what the *E* stands for." He started using that line with everybody who complained about the quality of our programming.

But to my mind, we were missing an opportunity to make a difference. When I came to BET full-time, I started talking to as many employees as I could, sitting down with people in the lunchroom and dropping in at the studios. I worked on the charity side of the business, doing events and giving speeches, and I started hosting dinner parties for the executives, and at every event, I'd talk with people about the bigger picture of what BET had become, as compared with what we wanted it to be.

As far as I could see, our network didn't have any kind of overarching structure or theme. Bob was just trying to fill hours with the cheapest programming he could, raking in more advertising dollars, increasing subscriber numbers, and racing toward an expected IPO. A decade after our founding, we were still the only TV option out there specifically for Black people, so the Black community wasn't inclined to criticize us too much, at least in the beginning. Which meant that maybe Bob's business strategy was smart in the short term—but in the longer term, I just didn't believe the network could sustain itself without some kind of vision. And it seemed obvious to me that Bob wasn't interested in any kind of "vision" that stretched beyond the bottom line.

During this period, I found myself talking a lot to Jeff Lee, who was now the head of programming and one of Bob's top executives. I knew I could trust him, and I'd bellyache to him all the time about what we were putting into the world. "Jeff, we have *got* to raise the quality of our programming," I would tell him. "We need to be educating, too, not just entertaining. This is getting ridiculous."

He agreed, but he also knew his directive from Bob was to focus on profit margins. People were afraid to cross Bob, because he didn't react well when others disagreed with him. He was a leader in the sense that he wielded his power without hesitation and he expressed his directives clearly. But in the deeper sense of the word, he wasn't really a leader at all. Yes, the company had survived its first decade, and since 1986 it had even managed to turn a profit. But the network didn't know what it was supposed to be, and what it was becoming was unsustainable.

I had hoped we could become the Black CNN, but *BET News* never really got off the ground. And I wasn't getting anywhere with seeking out new programming, so I finally just decided to create a higher-quality offering myself. I desperately wanted BET to show something that would counter the brain-dead sex and violence and misogyny of those music videos, and I wanted it to be specifically for young people. So I created *Teen Summit*.

My idea for *Teen Summit* was a one-hour show that would feature real students, not actors, talking about the issues affecting their lives. I wanted to find smart kids who were curious about the world and unafraid to express their opinions on serious subjects like drug use, family relationships, teen pregnancy, and AIDS, which was spreading like wildfire in the late 1980s but was still considered a taboo subject.

I started putting out feelers in the local community, calling schools and churches to ask whether they had any teenagers who might be right for the show. I wanted to build a roster of twenty-five good, upstanding students to be my "*Teen Summit* posse." "I need the best kids you have," I told the adults I talked to. And let me tell you, there was no shortage of nominations. Teachers, principals, and pastors were falling all over themselves to suggest students who fit the bill, and they seemed excited that we were creating this kind of show.

We decided to have the kids meet together on Fridays after school, to spitball about topics and bat around ideas. Then, on Saturday morning, they'd come into the studio and we'd shoot the show live, in front of a few dozen audience members, starting at noon. Working with a producer named Tony Regusters, we built a set that made it look like the kids were sitting on top of an inner-city building and hired a couple of fly girls to dance, to add some pop to the production. The whole thing had a fresh, exciting vibe. And the kids very quickly became the stars of the show.

I decided the show needed a host, but I didn't want an Oprah-style setup where the adult was leading the students in discussion. Instead, we hired a young woman named Lisa Johnson, who'd graduated from Temple University just two weeks before the show's launch. Lisa was smart, telegenic, and not much older than the kids in the posse, so she was perfect. She guided the conversation, and we had an 800 number for viewers to call with their questions or comments.

From the moment we started airing in September 1989, I was thrilled with *Teen Summit*. This was exactly what BET had been missing—an intelligent show featuring real talk about the issues that teenagers were facing. While it's true that BET kept showing those booty-shaking videos for hours on end during the week, at least young people knew that every Saturday at noon, they could tune in for something deeper. *Teen Summit* gave kids a safe place to learn about difficult topics, and we were often at the forefront of social change, such as when President Bill Clinton asked us to help lead a teen pregnancy prevention campaign.

But as much as I loved *Teen Summit*, Bob never got behind it. It seemed like he couldn't see the forest for the trees—and for him, the trees had leaves made of dollar bills. The only thing he had to say about the show was, "If it don't kill nothing, it don't get to eat," which was his way of warning that he'd cancel the show if its advertising support didn't improve. So, despite the fact that *Teen Summit* would go on to win multiple NAACP Image Awards, in addition to being nominated for CableACE Awards and even an Emmy, he was always threatening to shut it down. When he finally did decide to pull the plug in the mid-1990s, I just refused to accept it. I went out and persuaded the Kaiser Family Foundation to underwrite the show, so we wouldn't have to worry about ads.

Teen Summit was my baby, and I was proud of the way these kids dug fearlessly into tough topics. We talked about interracial relationships. We talked about bullying, about academic pressures, about what happens when parents split up. I remember one show where a mother in the audience almost passed out from shock at the brutal honesty her daughter was displaying. *Teen Summit* was a place where teenagers could lay it all out there, and from the letters and feedback we got, it truly made a difference for many young Black people of that era.

What Bob didn't seem to grasp was that it also made a difference for BET. People had started talking about how terrible our programming was, joking that BET stood for "Bad Entertainment Television." But I knew that the old saying was true—that Black companies, like Black people, have to be twice as good to get half the credit. You're constantly under a microscope. Like it or not, you're seen as representing your race. And I believe you have to live up to that. That's how I lead my companies today—and it started back when I was pushing Bob to live up to the expectations people had for BET.

Jeff Lee started calling me "the conscience of BET," because I was constantly focused on improving corporate integrity and putting out better programming. I believed that making money was nice, but not if it came at the expense of our souls. But to Bob, money was money, however you made it. He didn't have a conscience about the company, because he didn't have a conscience about himself; it just was not a priority for him. He always believed that the ends justified the means—that so as long as he made money for investors, nobody would care how he'd done it. To his credit, he worked long hours and poured himself into building the company. But unfortunately, his leadership method also involved threats and intimidation that would become even more overt as the company grew.

Bob's belief seemed to be that he had to cut corners and behave like a bully in order to make the company successful. My theory as a CEO is the opposite. Do right by people, respect them and treat them well, and the money will follow. In the twenty years I've been running my own businesses, that method has proved itself over and over again.

But in 1991, as BET started moving toward an initial public offering, I wasn't the one in charge. Bob was, and he was about to make another decision that would gut me to the core.

We had been working toward the IPO for several months, with Bear Stearns and First Boston underwriting it. By the fall of 1991, we had revenues of more than $50 million, and more than half of American homes with cable were subscribed to BET. Twelve years earlier, we had launched with just two hours of programming per week, and now we were on 24/7 and had near-total brand recognition among Black Americans. There was no doubt about it, BET was a huge success. And a successful IPO would make us even bigger.

A few days before the October 30 IPO, I said something to Bob about traveling up to New York for the event. "No, you're not coming," he said. Just like that.

"What do you mean?" I asked him. This was beyond ridiculous. I had been with BET from the very beginning, had signed for that first $15,000 loan, and had even sold my violin to keep the company afloat. I wasn't just Bob's wife—I was a cofounder of the company, the vice president of corporate affairs, and a major shareholder. I knew that a group of executives including Jeff Lee and Curtis Symonds was going up for the IPO, which was not only BET's biggest moment, it was actually historic. The IPO for BET Holdings Inc. would mark the first time ever that a Black-owned business debuted on the New York Stock Exchange.

Bob didn't care about any of that. He just didn't want me there. And so he simply said, "Sheila, you're not coming."

Now, what was I supposed to do with that? I guess I could have said, "Screw you, I'm coming," and gone up to New York and tried to bull my way onto the NYSE floor to take part in the event. But what good would that have done me? Bob didn't want me there. He wasn't the type to fight or yell, but he would have made me feel unwelcome and small. This was a huge victory for the company, but if I insisted on being there, he would find another way to humiliate me. Humiliation was Bob's specialty.

I was incredibly proud of what we'd done with BET. And that's what made Bob's casual slap-down so hurtful. Maybe I shouldn't have been surprised—after all, this was the same man who'd walked out on me on our wedding night. If he didn't want us to be together in our biggest personal moment, why would I have thought he'd want me by his side for our company's biggest moment? But somehow, despite all evidence to the contrary, I always thought that he would come around, that he would finally start treating me with some kind of respect. And then he'd find another way to insult or humiliate me. And I would just take it in, swallow my pain, feel it burn in my gut, and try to pretend it wasn't there. Over ... and over ... and over again.

As Bob knew I would, I just said, "Fine." I didn't go to New York but just kept my head down and went into work as usual on the day of the IPO.

We got updates throughout the day, and almost every time we looked, the stock was going higher. We opened at $17 a share, flew up to almost $24, and finally settled at $23.50. By the time the closing bell rang, BET was officially worth $472 million. Bob cashed out 375,000 of our shares, instantly providing us more than $6 million. But that wasn't all. He and I still owned 9.3 million shares, which were now worth $218 million. And because Bob had insisted on having different classes of shares, ours came with more votes. Even though we owned 46 percent of the stock, we controlled 56 percent of the vote. Which meant that we still controlled the company.

I was stunned. I knew how much stock we had, but I'd never dared to dream that it would be worth so much. For years, we had scratched and clawed and fought to create this company. And now all that hard work was paying off.

I tried to focus on everything good that happened that day—on the money we'd made for so many Black investors, on the value we had created, and on the history we had made. But it was tinged with a hollow feeling of sadness. As much as I kept hoping Bob and I would find our footing as a couple, with each day that passed, I was increasingly on my own. November 1, 1991, was a day of the highest highs and the lowest lows. Or so I thought, anyway. Because very soon, the lows were about to get even lower.

A couple of years earlier, we had moved from our Brandywine house into a slightly bigger home on Beach Drive in Northwest Washington. That's where I was one evening in January 1992 when I heard seven-year-old Paige cry out, "Mo-o-o-om!" I hurried into her room and found her in tears. She had just discovered that her pet gerbil had died.

Oh, how Paige loved that gerbil. She loved all animals, really—we had gone through iguanas, dogs, and cats, and she was now in the process of falling deeply in love with horses. But this gerbil was her baby. She liked to dress it in tiny clothes and have tea parties with it and her Barbies. And now her little friend was suddenly gone. Paige was bereft, sobbing on her bed, and as I looked around for a shoebox to put the gerbil in, I heard the doorbell ring.

I cracked the door open to find a young man standing there. "Are you Sheila Johnson?" he asked. I told him I was, and he thrust an envelope in my hands. "You've been served."

What was this about? I opened the envelope and pulled out a stack of papers. Apparently, Chickie Goodier, one of the three original employees at BET, was suing Bob. And I was one of the people her lawyers wanted to depose.

As Paige sniffled in her room, I flipped quickly through the paperwork. I wasn't surprised at what Chickie was asking for. She, Carol Coody, and Bob's sister Polly had all worked their butts off during those early years, when the company didn't have enough money to pay competitive salaries. (Which would explain why Polly might have ended up thinking it was okay to dip into the till for a little extra.) Chickie, who had come over from the National Cable Television Association, had received $40,000 a year—but now that BET had gone public, she was suing for a piece of the action. In her lawsuit, she claimed that in those early days, as a way of acknowledging how many hours they were putting in, Bob had promised her, Carol, and Polly shares in BET.

Back then, in the early 1980s, any thoughts of an IPO were just a distant dream. None of these three women were still with BET by the time we went public in 1991, but soon enough, Polly and Carol would file their own lawsuit claiming they, too, were owed shares.

Promising shares to early employees certainly sounded like something Bob might have done. I could imagine him smooth-talking his little team, trying to squeeze more hours of work out of them by promising a pot at the end of the rainbow. So that part of it didn't surprise me. What *did* surprise me was learning why Chickie Goodier had left BET. According to these papers I'd just been served, she had quit the company in 1982, just two years after we launched, because of a "personal relationship" with Bob that was "interfering" with the business.

Oh, noooo. My blood went cold. *No, no, no.* I'd had no idea Bob had been sleeping with Chickie. I mean, I had never really *noticed* Chickie, to be honest. She just seemed like a typical Washington, DC, white female executive, with her business suits and short hair. I knew she had traveled around with Bob to trade shows and sports events while we were getting BET off the ground, and I'd never thought anything about it. So this was how I learned about their three-year affair: by getting handed a subpoena and stumbling across that fact in the paperwork. And suddenly realizing, with a sick feeling in the pit of my stomach, that everyone else would now know too—if they hadn't already known, maybe even for many years.

Now Paige and I were both traumatized, although for completely different reasons. But while she was sad, I was angry.

It was bad enough that Bob was cheating on me. Did he really have to cheat with an *employee* of the company we founded? I could only imagine what the office gossip was like and how much of a fool people must have taken me for. It's not that I believed Bob would never have an affair. I had seen too much already to think that. If I was in denial, it wasn't about whether he'd do such a thing; it was more like a strange denial that anybody else might know he was doing it. I didn't want him to cheat, but maybe deep down, I must have known that he would. So I just didn't want to know about it. That was how I would get through. And now not only was it right here in black and white, but my humiliation was being put out there for the whole world to see.

I could feel the blood rushing to my face. I was furious, but I didn't want to add to Paige's stress, so I just clamped my mouth shut and dealt with the gerbil and my daughter's grief. But the minute Bob Johnson came through that door, he was going to *hear* from me.

When he walked in about an hour later, he was holding a box. He obviously knew what was coming, because he had brought me home an expensive necklace. I lit into him with a fury I had spent years tamping down. And Bob just took it. He was never a fighter or a shouter with me. He just stood there calmly, listening as I railed at him. He'd been gaslighting me for years about his goings-on with other women, always acting like I was talking crazy. But this time, he knew he was caught.

"Sheila, I am going to work this out," he said quietly. "I'm going to take care of this." What he didn't say was that he was sorry.

I hired a lawyer, who managed to get me out of giving a deposition in Chickie's case. More jewelry from Bob arrived, I guess in an effort to have me continue to keep my mouth shut. Then Carol Coody and Polly Johnson filed their lawsuits against Bob. He got deposed, they got deposed—and the details that started coming out just made everything even messier.

Like Chickie Goodier, Carol and Polly were suing for millions of dollars they believed Bob had promised them. In his deposition, Bob claimed that they had lost their rights to any stock when he fired them in 1985. In their depositions, they claimed they were never fired but instead chose to quit.

Polly testified that Bob was verbally abusive to her after she confronted him about "dating the staff." And then she described the same kind of gaslighting that Bob had done to me. "If I didn't do exactly what he wanted me to do, if I wasn't exactly like him, he was going to come back and tell me that I was crazy, or I had a problem, or I didn't like white people, or he was going to demean me in some kind of way," she testified. This was exactly the same playbook he used with me.

Carol Coody offered similar testimony, saying that Bob created an unbearable work environment. She claimed that Bob had asked her to spy on Polly and said that despite "superior" marks on her evaluations, she felt she had no choice but to resign. She also mentioned Bob's affairs, testifying that they "were demoralizing everyone at BET."

The two lawsuits dragged on for months, until finally Bob agreed to settle before they went to trial. He paid $900,000 each to Carol and Polly, and more than $2 million to Chickie Goodier. Four million dollars, family ties destroyed, a public airing of his infidelities and bullying, and a black eye to the reputation of BET. I had put up with so much to this point, but when would it be *too* much?

I never talked with my mother about what was happening with Bob. I just couldn't. I'd seen what she went through with my father, and I was embarrassed to have gotten myself in the same damn situation, of having a husband who strayed. I also knew what had happened to my mother when my father left. She was stuck with two children, no money, a crushing burden of shame, and the humiliation of being cast out from their social circle. I was terrified the same thing would happen to me if I let Bob get away. No matter how badly he treated me, the more I clung to the marriage.

There were really only two people I talked to about my situation, and they had very different reactions. Susan Starrett had sniffed out Bob from the very beginning, and she had tried to persuade me not to marry him. When I told her about his affair with Chickie Goodier, she just sighed. "Sheila, he is not worthy of you," she said, for the umpteenth time. I thought of the question she'd asked me more than twenty years earlier: "Are you sure he's the quality of person you want?" Back then, I had truly thought he was. And now that I knew he wasn't, I was too terrified to do anything about it.

The other person I talked to was Alice Queen. I had known her back at Sidwell, one of the only other Black people on staff when I was teaching. I liked and trusted Alice, who sometimes helped me take care of the kids and always had my back. But when I told her about Bob's latest affair, she lowered her chin and gave me a look. "Sheila," she said, "whatever you do, you cannot leave him."

"Alice, I'm miserable," I told her. "I can't take this anymore."

"Listen," she said. "You and Bob represent the Black community. You have got to just hang in there." I looked at her, tears streaming down my face. She leaned closer and then said, "This is normal. This is just what men do."

There was so much history, so much social and cultural pressure, in these few sentences. Yes, Alice cared about me, but not as much as she cared about what white society might think if the king and queen of Black media were to split up in a scandal. There are certain unwritten rules within Black culture, and one of them is that you don't criticize your own. Bob could have been sleeping with fifty other women and doing it right out on the lawn of the National Mall, but *we have to stand by him*, because he's the head of BET! We don't want one of our most successful businessmen to be tarnished, because that tarnishes our whole community. So we just collectively turn our heads, eager to keep people on pedestals they didn't deserve to be on in the first place.

Bob put his own spin on it in an interview with C-SPAN in 1992, the year the lawsuits were filed. "I don't want to be seen as a hero to younger people," he said. "I want to be seen as a good, solid business guy who goes out and does a job, and that job is to build a business . . . In the Black community, there's always a rush to say you've got to be a role model, you've got to be a hero and all of this. Well, I think we probably need less hero worship." He made a point-blank racial comparison: "There are probably literally thousands of white businessmen . . . who never get asked, 'Are you a hero?'" There's some truth to that. But by the same token, Bob was basically using it to declare his right to do whatever he wanted to do.

Alice Queen wasn't the only one who urged me to stay with Bob for the greater good. Over the years, so many older Black women said the same damn thing. I'd be at an event, and someone would suddenly appear at my elbow, lean close, and whisper, "Girl, just bite your lip and keep on going." Or, "Stay strong! We need you both!" It's not like people thought Bob could do no wrong. They *knew* he was doing wrong. But they believed that was an acceptable price to pay for the things he was doing right. And it was up to me to just keep my mouth shut and hold my head high. It was up to me to take one for the whole Black team.

People put so much pressure on me, so much guilt, that even if I'd *had* the courage to leave Bob at that time, I probably couldn't have gone through with it. But I didn't have the courage. Not yet. Believe it or not, there was a whole lot more I'd have to go through before that happened.

In the meantime, BET was about to go through some things too.

Not long after I got served with that subpoena, I was down in the garage at BET when Delmar, one of our maintenance guys, walked up. "Mrs. Johnson," he said, "do you have a minute to talk?"

Delmar was the main manager of our facility, a young Black man who kept track of deliveries and worked closely with the cleaning staff. I liked him, because he was sharp and kept an eagle eye on everything. But I'm not sure how well others in the building treated him, because people tend to look right past maintenance staff. When I was in school, my mother taught me to always make friends with the janitors, because if you ever need help getting into the building or getting supplies, they're the ones who can help. And that's true. But the more important point was that maintenance staff deserve the same kind of respect that any employee does, no matter their position in the company.

I had always been friendly with Delmar, so I wasn't surprised when he approached me. But then I noticed that he was sweating.

"Delmar, is everything okay?" I asked. "What's going on?"

"Something's not right," he said. "There's things going out the back door."

I asked him what he meant. "Computers, other equipment," he said. "Somebody's stealing them." He looked me in the eye. "I'm just telling you what I'm seeing. I thought you and Mr. Johnson should know."

"Thank you, Delmar," I said. And then I thought for a moment about what to do next.

The truth was, I had already mentioned to Bob that I thought something fishy was going on at BET. Our CFO, Antonia Duncan, had started buying up real estate in the DC area, even though she was making only $170,000 a year—a good salary, but certainly not enough to become a real estate mogul. When she bought a restaurant on Connecticut Avenue, I said, "Bob, there is something really strange going on here." But he just ignored me, in the same way he'd ignored me seven years earlier when I asked why his paychecks were going up and down.

There in the garage, I made a snap decision. "I think you need to tell Mr. Johnson yourself," I told Delmar. I gave him our home address and asked him to bring whatever documentation he had that might prove items were being stolen.

That Sunday, Delmar showed up at our front door. He was so nervous that he was actually trembling. "I don't want to get fired," he said. "But here's what's going on." He handed over a stack of papers, then turned and walked quickly away. Bob took the papers, which documented the equipment and assets coming in and out of BET, then sat at the table reading them over and over again, rubbing his temples. "I can't believe it," he mumbled, then sat back in his chair.

The following week, Bob shut down the BET office so an independent investigator could look into the thefts. And as it turned out, Antonia had done more than just steal a few computers. She had made off with nearly $2 million. For the second time in seven years, the person in charge of BET's money was brazenly stealing it.

Antonia Duncan was fired in September 1992, and she pleaded guilty and ended up doing jail time for her crimes. But the cloud that had fallen over BET persisted even after she was gone. It's a terrible feeling to trust someone and then to have that trust publicly betrayed. All you can do after that is keep moving forward . . . at least until the next time it happens.

Eight

GASLIT

From the outside looking in, our lives must have seemed pretty glamorous after the IPO. All those years of hard work, of fighting to make BET profitable and grow the company, had finally paid off. We were able to buy a new house in the Forest Hills neighborhood of DC, and a house in Rehoboth Beach. We also got heavily into philanthropy, giving money to organizations like the United Negro College Fund, the Levine School of Music (now Levine Music), and Howard University. And we got involved with Bill Clinton's presidential campaign in 1992, hosting fundraisers at our home.

Through all these activities, our profile as a couple continued to rise. Bob and I got invitations to events in New York and Los Angeles, where we were able to meet and get to know celebrities like Denzel Washington and Oprah Winfrey. Magazines and newspapers bumped up their coverage of us. After the 1992 election, we started spending time at the White House, getting to know Bill and Hillary Clinton and having the honor of attending events there.

I hoped that after making it this far, Bob might finally be happy, and that after settling those lawsuits, maybe he would behave a little better. At the very least, I hoped that he would be kinder to me after putting me through the very public humiliation of the Chickie Goodier affair. With all that jewelry, he had clearly been trying to smooth things over, so maybe now he might actually mend his ways and be the man I had always believed he could be.

Instead, he went in the other direction. He became emotionally abusive and downright mean. He had done this off and on over the years, but now he took it to a new level. It was as if the more successful he got in business, the more he needed to cut me down.

"You're too fat," he would say. Or, "Why do you wear your hair like that? It looks ugly." Or, "You look ridiculous in that outfit." Some other woman was always prettier, was always smarter, had gone to a better college than me, had a better figure. And he wanted me to know about it. He would insult and degrade me in front of anyone—employees, friends, even our kids. But instead of telling him where he could put those insults, or at least ignoring them, I took them to heart. They pierced right through me.

No matter how mean he was to me, I kept trying to please him. When he said I was fat, I worked to lose weight—and then he said I was too thin. When he said he didn't like my hair, I cut it—and then he said it was too short. If he didn't like an outfit, I changed it. I never had the courage to stand up to him and say, *Enough*. Years later, I would realize that this was the same dynamic I had with my father after he left, when I'd actually sent him Christmas presents after he abandoned my brother and me.

My god, I was always, *always* trying to please Bob. And I couldn't seem to recognize that no matter how hard I tried, that was never going to happen. He would just find something else to criticize me about, because the criticism was the whole point.

Sometime during this period, I decided to buy myself a camera and study photography. I loved going out and taking pictures, as it felt like an escape. I started printing some of my photos, and even framed a few and hung them in our home. And Bob just dumped all over me for it. "You need to stop with that," he'd say, in front of guests. "You're not a photographer. Who do you think you are?" He did the same with my music. I was still playing the violin regularly, and occasionally that fact would come up in a cocktail party conversation. Once, someone even asked me to play a little bit, and I obliged. And Bob just couldn't stand it. "You think you're all that, just because you play the violin?" he'd say. No matter what I did, he was determined to slap it down. He couldn't bear it if anyone paid attention to me rather than him.

After a while, I was trying so hard to be what I thought Bob wanted me to be, I began to lose sight of who I actually was. I constantly felt like a failure around him, always on edge, waiting for the next insult. It was like a game for him, some kind of cruel Whack-a-Mole, where if I ever had a good feeling pop up, he'd rush to knock it back down. I'd get upset with him when he behaved that way—but deep down, I wondered if he was right. Did I actually look as embarrassing as he said? Was there something wrong with me? The ground beneath me was shifting so violently, I never knew where I stood, or even how to keep standing.

In a strange way, I started to feel invisible—as if the point of my existence was to support Bob and BET. And so I just put my head down and kept working, raising our children, and trying to be the best wife, mother, and company executive I could.

And then, stranger things began happening.

I was at work one day, walking through a hallway in our new corporate building in Southeast DC, when an employee whispered, "I'm praying for you," as I passed by. *You're what, now?* What was this about? A few days later, someone else said the same thing. Why was everybody at BET praying for me all of a sudden?

Unfortunately, I had a hunch about what the answer might be— and soon enough, I overheard a conversation that seemed to confirm it. I was standing by Bob's office one morning and heard his assistant making travel plans for him. I don't remember where he was going, but he'd be traveling with BET's president and COO, Debra Lee. The assistant was on the phone with somebody, making sure that Bob and Debra would have connecting rooms in the hotel.

Now, if you're on a business trip and you need to see a colleague in the room next to yours, it's easy enough to go out into the hallway, walk two steps, and knock on their door. The only reason to have a connecting door *inside* is if you don't want anyone else to see when you're coming and going. So when I overheard that little snippet of conversation, I began to suspect what anybody would—that Bob and Debra were having an affair. This wasn't a big leap to make, as I'd already noticed a few other things that aroused my suspicion. They traveled together all the time, and their body language around one another had become oddly intimate. My antennae were already up, and the assistant's comments felt like confirmation of what was going on.

This, finally, would be the straw that broke my back. I had known Debra Lee for more than a decade. We had a friendly relationship. I had supported her throughout her rise at BET, and she had been in our home for dinners many times. I knew her husband, Randall

Coleman, and her kids even went to school with my kids. I wasn't 100 percent sure what was happening between her and Bob, but if it turned out that they were having an affair, and everyone at the company knew it, I did know one thing: that this would be the cruelest, most painful cut of all.

Debra joined the company back in 1986, just after the Polly fiasco, and at a time when Bob decided he needed to bulk up our legal team. She had the kind of pedigree that impressed him, with degrees from Brown and from Harvard Law School. She had been working at Steptoe & Johnson, one of DC's big white-shoe law firms, and Bob wanted to bring her in as BET's general counsel.

After I met her, Bob asked me what I thought, and I said she'd be a good hire. We definitely needed more lawyers, and she seemed competent and had a good track record. And I was always supportive of having women in top executive positions, as so many upper-level jobs traditionally went to men. When Debra started at BET, I was still running my music business. But she and I always had a friendly rapport, and I got to know her better when I joined the company full-time in 1989.

Although she was hired as general counsel, her role soon expanded. When Bob decided to launch a magazine in 1991—*YSB*, which stood for "Young Sisters and Brothers"—he put Debra in charge of it. She had never run that kind of project before, and although it did well at first, it soon was losing the company close to $2 million a year. By 1996, it was gone. Bob didn't seem to mind, though, as he kept adding projects to Debra's plate, including managing the construction of our new headquarters building.

In March 1996, Bob made a decision that shocked many on the executive staff: he named Debra Lee president and COO of the company, elevating her ahead of longtime executives such as Curtis Symonds and Jeff Lee. People couldn't believe it. The move came out of the blue, and a few of the executives went to Bob's office to confront him about it. Bob just told them that he'd made up his mind and the decision was final. Debra was now the number two person at BET, positioned to take over the company whenever Bob stepped down.

By this time, Bob and Debra were already traveling everywhere together. And while Bob had previously traveled with Curtis and Jeff, that wasn't really happening anymore. I don't know exactly when the affair started, but I can tell you that I didn't suspect anything when Bob named her COO. In fact, I was so thrilled for her, I even bought her a bouquet of flowers. I carried them into her office, a big smile on my face. "Congratulations, Debra!" I said. "This is really cool."

Thinking about that moment all these years later, I'm flooded with emotions all over again. I feel embarrassed. Humiliated. Disappointed. And angry. It's possible that the affair hadn't started yet. But even if that didn't happen until later, it's galling to think about how happy I was for Debra that day, how supportive I'd always been of her career at BET, and how she repaid me by getting into bed with my husband.

After I overheard the assistant's comments about connecting rooms, I confronted Bob. "Why are you traveling so much with Debra Lee?" I asked.

"Sheila, come on," he said, shaking his head. "She's COO of the company. We have to travel together."

"Then why do you need connecting hotel rooms?" I said, my

voice rising. I was furious and not in the mood for any more of his gaslighting. But that is, of course, exactly what I got.

"You're being ridiculous," he said. "There's nothing going on. Just calm down." And, "You're imagining things again." And, "You really need to get some professional help." He looked me straight in the eye as he said all of this, which of course made me doubt myself again. Could anybody really be that good at lying? Was it at all possible he was actually telling the truth? I felt stuck: If he *was* lying, did that mean I was married to a sociopath? On the other hand, if he was telling the truth, did that mean I was paranoid and delusional? No matter which way I turned, the outcome was horrible. I began to feel like I was losing my mind.

I needed to get out of Washington, DC, out of my bubble of misery and away from the prying eyes and "prayers" of colleagues. Fortunately, I had found the perfect place to escape to—a piece of land nestled in the lush, gorgeous countryside between The Plains and Middleburg, Virginia, about a ninety-minute drive west of DC.

Our daughter, Paige, now in middle school, had turned her childhood love of horses into a budding career as an elite equestrian. As she got more serious about riding, we started taking her to competitions, many of which took place in this stretch of Virginia's horse country. We drove her to the Upperville Colt and Horse Show, the oldest horse show in the United States, and the Warrenton Pony Show. And every time I'd drive down those rural roads, past lush green pastures with the Blue Ridge Mountains looming in the distance, I felt like I was being transported to another place and time. The low stone walls and centuries-old homes brought the English countryside to mind, and life out there seemed so much more peaceful and inviting than the hell I was living through in DC.

The more time I spent in the rolling hills and historic old towns of this area, the deeper I fell in love with it. Paige's horse shows became my escape, and I looked forward to those weekend trips like a starving person anticipates a meal. Then one afternoon, as I was driving down Zulla Road just outside Middleburg, I noticed an old stone house that had a spectacular view of the Blue Ridge Mountains. There was just something about that piece of land, and that view, that deeply moved me. *That's where I want to live*, I thought.

I called a local real estate agent, Phil Thomas, and asked whether the place was for sale. He told me it had recently been bought by a polo-playing businessman named Bill Ylvisaker. "So, it's not currently for sale," he said. My heart sank. But then Phil added, "Although . . . anything's for sale if you can convince someone to sell it."

The parcel of land, which was called Cotswold Farm, was 168 acres, with a pond, rolling hills, and a nineteenth-century stone house. Bill kept his polo ponies at the property, so I couldn't imagine he'd be willing to sell—especially so soon after he'd bought it. But I really wanted that beautiful farm. When Bob and I approached him, we did so with an offer that was meant to motivate. And it did. Bill sold us the property in 1996, and I started making plans to renovate the main house, to expand it and make it my own.

There was only one problem. I didn't love the name Cotswold Farm, because it sounded too much like Callanwolde, the name of an estate in the Pat Conroy novel *The Prince of Tides* and the nickname of a man who rapes a child in the book. I definitely didn't want to be reminded of that all the time, so I started to think about renaming the farm. Then Phil Thomas told me that the parcel had previously been owned by Bruce Sundlun, the former governor of Rhode Island and a World War II hero—and that he had called the place Salamander Farm, after the code name he'd been given during the war.

Why "Salamander"? I did a little more digging and learned the story behind the name. Bruce had been flying a mission over Belgium in 1943 when his airplane was shot down. It crashed into a turnip field in Nazi-occupied territory, and of ten men on the plane, five died, four were captured—and only Bruce escaped. He made his way on foot and by bicycle all the way to France. There he got involved with the French Resistance, and he continued to fight the Nazis until the end of the war. The French gave him the "Salamander" nickname because according to legend, the salamander is the only animal that can walk through fire and survive.

Walk through fire . . . and survive. I couldn't believe it when I heard this description; it was absolutely perfect. The moment I learned that detail, I decided to restore the name Salamander Farm to my Middleburg home. Bruce Sundlun was still living, so I called him to ask his blessing, which he readily gave. Later, of course, I would also name my resort and my company after the salamander. But that was all in the future. For now, I was focused on only one thing. I was walking through fire, and I needed to find a way to survive.

There was a double-wide trailer on the land, so I was able to spend time out there with Paige and Brett even while the house and grounds were being renovated. As often as possible, I'd make the drive out to Salamander Farm, as the fresh air and the views of the Shenandoah always calmed me. I kept working at BET and kept my primary residence with Bob in Washington. But getting out to Middleburg was the first step in saving myself—even though life was still destined to get worse before it would get better.

• • •

One night in 1997, I was at our home in DC, getting ready to go with Bob to an event at the White House. I had bought a stunning red gown for the occasion and had taken much of the afternoon to prepare. I'd gotten my hair fixed, done my makeup, put on the dress and some jewelry I'd chosen to match. I felt good, and I was excited to go to the White House. It doesn't matter if you've never been there or if you've been there many times; it's always an honor and a thrill to join the president and first lady for an event.

I came downstairs and found Miss Mary in the kitchen. Mary Henderson was an older Black woman who had worked many years earlier as a janitor at BET. Back then, I'd noticed that she had problems lifting things and doing the physical work of cleaning, so one day I said, "Why don't you just come work with us at home?" And she did. She was an amazing cook, and she helped care for Brett and Paige from the time they were in diapers. Mary loved those kids like they were her own, and they loved her right back. She was a part of our family and had been for years.

Mary and I sat in the kitchen chatting as I waited for Bob to get home. We had a driver waiting to take us to the White House, but for some reason Bob was running late. The clock kept ticking, and I could see Mary looking sideways toward the door. Where was he?

Finally, just as I was worrying that we'd miss the start of the event, Bob came breezing into the house. He ran upstairs, put on his tuxedo, and came back down to the kitchen. When I stood to go, he looked me up and down and said, "I am not going out with you looking like that." And then he turned and strode out the door, leaving me standing there, my face burning and tears starting to sting my eyes.

Mary stomped her foot so hard, I thought she might put it through the floor. "Child," she said, her nostrils flaring, "that man is a *snake*." Mary was from Mississippi, and she had a southern sense of propriety about her. But while she normally held her tongue about things she witnessed in our home, Bob had finally gone too far. She said, "I'm telling you; I had a dream about a snake, and I couldn't see its face. But *he* is the snake."

I started crying, out of sheer anger, frustration, and helplessness. I felt like such a fool, standing there in the kitchen in my gown and jewelry. Mary's eyes, which had flared with fire a moment ago, turned soft. "Honey," she said, "you have been through hell. This man is putting you through hell." She was a big woman, and when she wrapped me in her arms, I felt so small I might as well have disappeared. I appreciated that she was looking out for me, but I felt so humiliated I could barely speak.

One of the strangest things about Bob's behavior was that after pulling something like this, he'd always act like everything was fine the next time he saw me. I went to bed miserable that night, but when Bob came home hours later, he was singing a little tune. He did this all the time—I'd see the headlights in the driveway, and when the front door opened I could hear him humming or singing happily to himself, like life was just his own personal little cabaret.

Even when I would get angry at him, he'd either respond lightly or just ignore me. He never yelled back; instead, he'd just shut down. In some ways, that was even worse. If only he had engaged, it would at least have shown me that he had some kind of emotional connection to what was happening. But he never did. It was like talking to a brick wall. "Bob," I'd say, "you've got to *listen* to me. I need you to hear what I'm saying!" He'd just look at me, his eyes cold. And if I cried, he'd just turn on his heel and walk away.

Bob abandoned me both emotionally and physically; we were no longer living as husband and wife. He wasn't present in any way that mattered. Yet I knew he was having a ball out there in the world, screwing other women, enjoying his status as the BET big man, and pretending like all of this was absolutely normal. It was obvious that I didn't matter to him, and now I wondered if I ever had.

Strangely enough, I wasn't the only one he was abandoning. At around this same time, he started tossing his most loyal BET executives to the curb. Increasingly, the only person who mattered to Bob Johnson was Bob Johnson—and maybe Debra Lee. The rest of us would just end up as casualties along the way.

By 1997, Bob had decided he didn't want BET to be a public company anymore. The stock had done well in the six years since the IPO, but he didn't like having to answer to investors for whatever new directions he wanted to take the company in. We had a strong TV and media presence, but now Bob wanted to branch out in a million other ways, from BET-branded credit cards, to restaurants, to clothing lines, to nightclubs and casinos and beyond.

That year, the annual executive retreat was to be held in Palm Beach, Florida. A few weeks beforehand, Bob pulled the top executives—Jeff Lee, Curtis Symonds, Janis Thomas, Debra Lee, James Ebron, and the new CFO, William Gordon—together in one of the conference rooms at BET. I wasn't there, but I heard about what happened later. Some of the people in the room also talked to

Forbes writer Brett Pulley, who ended up putting the details in a book he later wrote called *The Billion Dollar BET*.

As the meeting got started, Bob announced that he had a request. In order to take the company private again, he had to buy back a big chunk of stock, which he planned to do with the help of John Malone. About one-third of BET's shares were in the hands of investors, including the executives in the room, who had been granted a total of around $40 million in stock options over the years. Worried about the cost of buying back all those shares, Bob made a shocking suggestion. He asked the executives if they'd be willing to give back half of their stock options—in other words, to just voluntarily hand over to the company about $20 million that they were owed.

People were understandably confused. "Will we be owners in the new company?" Jeff Lee asked. Meaning, were they going to get a piece of it—or anything at all—in return? Or did Bob think they'd just hand over millions of dollars' worth of stock out of the goodness of their hearts?

Bob told them that they'd be doing this for the good of the company, so that BET could go private and pursue new paths. William Gordon, the newest executive and only white man in the room, said outright that he wouldn't do it. Bob told him that was fine—and then he began pushing the others harder to accept the arrangement. He urged them to do it for BET, but this was just too much. In the end, they all said no, insisting that if Bob and John Malone wanted to buy back their stock, they had to pay what it was worth.

As it turned out, though, not all the executives said no. Days later, at an all-hands meeting attended by hundreds of BET employees, Bob announced that Debra Lee had volunteered to give back half her shares. This came as a surprise, but what he said next stunned everyone. "In return," he said, "she will own two percent of the new company."

Jeff Lee, Curtis Symonds, and the others were floored. Bob had never said anything about offering a piece of the private company in exchange for giving back shares. It certainly looked like Debra Lee had gotten preferential treatment, a sentiment Brett Pulley echoed in *The Billion Dollar BET*: "If there was any question in their minds before, they now knew for sure that Debra Lee was valued by the boss far more than any of the rest of them."

Later that month, those same top executives headed down to Palm Beach for the retreat, along with, for the first time, a group of lower-level executives. As with the IPO, Bob made it clear that he didn't want me there, and by that time, I felt so disconnected from him and from the company that I just said, "Fine." But when I heard later what happened, I couldn't believe my ears.

Bob chartered a boat to take everyone out on a dinner cruise. Once everyone was on board and the boat had sailed out into the Atlantic Ocean, he began giving his "state of the union" about the company. But instead of focusing on the business, he started criticizing the five executives who had declined to give back their shares. He said he was "not sure about their commitment moving forward," then told the lower-level people on board, "This may be your opportunity to step up." He was hanging out to dry the very people who'd been with him the longest, the ones who had worked their tails off for years to turn BET into the company it now was.

Curtis Symonds had heard enough. He swore at Bob, then told him that if he had issues with the executives, he should speak with them privately. Bob pushed back, and soon everybody was shouting. Jeff Lee, who had joined BET way back in 1982, said, "Bob, I've walked through fire for this company!" Debra Lee, of course, had no complaints, because Bob had made sure she was taken care of. But none of the other top executives could understand why he was throwing them under the bus for holding on to the rewards they had rightfully earned.

They didn't know it at the time, but this was the beginning of the end for most of those executives. Over the next couple of years, each one got demoted or reassigned, and eventually they all either resigned from the company or were fired.

Bob and Debra remained alone at the top of the company, and after a while, they seemed to feel powerful enough that they didn't even care who knew about their affair. They'd have intimate dinners for two at the Four Seasons, and I was told that once, on a business trip, she actually came down to breakfast at a hotel wearing his shirt. At public events he'd stick by her side, guiding her around with his hand on her back, just like he used to do with me at those Kappa Alpha Psi parties back in college. By now, the "I'm praying for you" whispers at BET had turned into full-on hot gossip, with employees eagerly trading the latest Bob-and-Debra sightings. They were now brazen enough to behave however they liked, regardless of whether or not I was present.

For years, Bob and I had hosted the company Christmas party at our home, a tradition I loved and one that I always worked hard to make perfect. But now, he informed me that Debra would be taking over the hosting. What made it feel even weirder was that she'd be holding the party at our old house on Broad Branch Road, which Bob had sold to Debra and her husband when we moved into our new home.

Although I was unhappy that Debra was taking my place as host, I decided to make the best of it. I put on a blue St. John dress and made my way over to her house, which was just around the corner from ours. Entering the front hallway, I greeted a few people and then saw Bob standing in another room. I started walking toward him, but as soon as he saw me, he turned, put his arm around Debra's shoulders, and guided her away from me and into another part of the house. Everybody who was standing nearby saw, and immediately understood, what was happening. I mean, Bob might as well have given me the finger; that's how obvious it was.

Debra's husband was standing there, too, and he and I exchanged glances. I couldn't believe he would sit there and watch as another man squired his wife around in his own house, but he just looked down at the floor and then shuffled off to another room. Standing there in my blue dress, embarrassed and alone, I turned around and headed straight for the door. I held my head up until I got outside, and then I burst into tears.

One night not long after that, Bob and I got into a fight about what was happening in our marriage. As usual, he didn't want to talk about it, so instead of engaging with me, he turned and walked out of the house. He didn't come back for hours, and I sat up half the night crying, wondering what on earth I was going to do. Something had to give, but I didn't know what. I just felt so vulnerable, so scared of what would happen if I left him.

I didn't have the courage to leave. And even if I somehow found the courage, I didn't know *how* to leave. What would happen to me and the kids if I walked out? Would Bob leave me high and dry, as my father had done to my mother? Bob always presented himself as the face of BET; would he claim he'd built the company himself and try to cut me off financially if I left him? Every time I thought about walking out, I kept seeing visions of my mother curled up on the kitchen floor, wailing and drooling, an empty shell of a woman. My father had put her through hell, and despite having vowed that I'd never let a man do that to me, I was about two words away from curling up on the kitchen floor just as she had.

My mind went around and around. I truly felt like there was no way out of my situation. I couldn't stay with him, but I was terrified to leave him. Lying there in bed, I felt the full weight of all my bad decisions, all my humiliations, all my failures, crushing in on me in the dark of the night. I began to wonder whether this life was still worth living. I had never had suicidal thoughts before. But I just couldn't see a path forward—and the path I was on was killing me.

The next day, afraid of the thoughts I was having, I knew I had to get out of the house and do something. I drove over to Foxhall Square, a little shopping mall in northwest DC, to buy some toys for Brett and Paige, thinking that might calm me down. I walked into a boutique store there called Tree Top Toys and began looking around. Brett was ten at the time, and Paige was fourteen, and as I stood there thinking about them, I felt overwhelmed with emotion. I loved my kids so much. They were my life. I was at the end of my rope, but I had to do something—for them. But how?

Right there in the store, amid all the colorful toys and games and stuffed animals, I finally fell completely apart. I started crying, but not in a subtle, tears-coming-down-my-face way. I was *sobbing*, hunched over, my face in my hands. I could barely catch my breath, and my head started pounding. It got so bad that the woman at the register came out from behind the counter and into the store to make sure I was okay.

"Can I help you?" she asked nervously. "Is there someone I can call?"

For a moment, I couldn't even speak. Then I managed to croak, "I'm okay. I'm just going through a really rough time. I'm just really unhappy." She stood with me while I struggled to compose myself, and I finally said, "I'm sorry. I've got to get out of here." She nodded, and I walked back out of the store.

That's the moment when I knew. I had to leave Bob, because I couldn't continue to live like this. Being unable to take care of myself was one thing, but I had two kids. I had to find a way to move forward, some way, somehow. Because whatever lay ahead couldn't possibly be worse than what I was going through now.

I drove home that day determined to save myself.

And then, Bob fired me from BET.

Nine

PRAYER PATH

I suppose I should have known that Bob would push me out of the company. He was doing the same thing with his other top executives, either firing them or asking them to resign. From the moment I confronted him about his affair with Debra Lee, it was only a matter of time. He didn't want anyone who'd complained about her to remain in the company—which he seemed to believe he could run just fine with only his COO and apparent mistress at his side.

But somehow it still came as a shock when he looked at me one morning and said, "Sheila, you're done. I need you to pack up your office."

I'm sorry, what? I stared at him, unable to believe he would actually go that far. Who fires his own wife, the cofounder of their company? This was getting absurd. And then he said, "Make sure you clear out on a Sunday. We don't need everybody seeing it."

So he wanted me to empty out my office when nobody was looking and then just stop coming into work, and that would be it—

the end of my twenty-year involvement with the company we had started together. I don't even think any announcement was made, or if it was, I never heard about it. Because once Bob fired me, I had no interest in ever walking into that building again. I had given my blood, sweat, and tears to BET and had worked tirelessly to try to make it the kind of company we could be proud of. But with this final indignity, I was done.

I had a driver who'd been working for me for several years at that point, a kind and protective man named George Walker. He said, "Mrs. Johnson, don't worry about this. I will take care of it." George called a couple of guys, and the three of them went to my office the following Sunday, boxed up all my belongings, and delivered them to me in Middleburg.

Among my things were some family photos I'd had made about a year earlier. Relations between Bob and me were beyond terrible at that point, but I thought Paige and Brett might like to have a family portrait while we were actually still a family. I made arrangements with a photographer, and on the day of the appointment, the kids and I got dressed and came down to sit for the session.

But Bob refused to take part. "You all go ahead," he said. "I'm not doing it." No matter how much we tried to cajole him, he would not sit for even a single picture. The photographer ended up making portraits with just the three of us, and I had them at home and at work. I loved having photos of the kids and me, but people would look at the portraits and say, "Where's Bob?" And I'd just say, "He wasn't available that day."

Around that same time, I went to visit my mother in Illinois and brought her some of those portraits, along with a few other photos. As we sat at the kitchen table, she flipped through them and then looked at me, her eyebrows raised. "Why isn't Bob in any of these pictures?" she asked.

"Oh, you know . . . he's busy," I said, not meeting her eye. "He travels a lot." When I dared to glance at her, the look she was giving me could have cut through steel.

"Sheila," she said. "Tell me the truth."

I took a deep breath. I loved my mother, but even as bad as my marriage had gotten, I still hadn't told her about his affairs, the gaslighting, and the insults. I didn't want to burden her, and I didn't want to bring back memories of how my dad had treated her. And truth be told, I was embarrassed.

But that look told me that she wasn't taking "He's busy" as an answer. So I said, "Mom, I'm just going through a rough patch."

My mother put her hand on mine and said, "Talk to me."

I shook my head. "I don't want to talk about it right now," I told her. I was wearing my shame like a cloak and had been for so many years. I just couldn't get out from under it, and until I found a way to do that, there was no way I could talk to her about what was happening in my life.

The one person I continued to talk to about everything was Susan Starrett. More than three decades after she had first walked into my life, Susan continued to be a steady, solid presence. For many years, she was the one person I spoke with openly and honestly about what was going on between Bob and me. And she always made herself available in my times of need.

Susan was there for me over the Thanksgiving holiday in 1999, when Bob was particularly cruel to me at our family meal. I had recently joined the international board of the National Center for Missing and Exploited Children, and I was telling Brett and Paige about the work we were doing. Bob said, "Oh my god, here we go," his voice dripping with sarcasm. "Aren't you just something, saving the world like that."

Humiliating me in private was one thing, but doing it in front of our kids was another. So I finally stood up for myself. I told Bob to get out, that he wasn't welcome at the table if he was going to insult me. And sure enough, he pushed his chair back, put down his napkin, and walked out the door. Another meal, another moment, another day, ruined. All I could think was, *This* has *to be the last one.*

I called Susan Starrett that night, and she and I talked until the sun rose. She helped me to see that staying with Bob was actually damaging to the kids, and that my efforts to hold the family together would do more harm than good in the long run. When I finally said aloud the words that I had dreaded for years—"I've got to get a divorce"—she responded with sympathy and grace. "I think you're seeing this clearly," she told me. "And I support you."

Finally, after all these agonizing years, I was ready.

I started pulling together the financial records and information on our assets that I'd need to file for divorce. I was the one who always paid the bills and kept track of our accounts, so this wasn't hard to do. I wanted to have everything in order for when I approached a divorce lawyer, because I needed to make absolutely sure that I wouldn't be left high and dry like my mother had been.

But there was one asset that Bob and I owned that I had much less control over: our BET stock. BET was a privately owned company now, and we owned more than 60 percent of it. We obviously couldn't just sell off all those shares, but I couldn't stand the thought of having my finances still tangled up with his even after a divorce. I needed to make a clean break and be done with everything associated with Bob Johnson. I deserved my half of those assets. And the only way to get it was by selling the company.

The irony is, after all those years of agonizing and of feeling paralyzed by fear at the thought of leaving Bob, I don't even remember the specific conversation when I finally told him I wanted a divorce. I'm pretty sure we were in the house in DC, but I can't even swear to that. All I remember is that I told him, "You've got to sell the company."

And he just said, "Okay." He didn't fight it. In fact, he didn't even bat an eye. Maybe he knew it was time too.

Then he said, "We need to talk to the kids."

We got Paige and Brett together, and the four of us sat down for what I was afraid would be a very difficult conversation. I had no idea what Bob might have to say about all this or how the kids would take it.

"Your mother and I are getting a divorce," he said. Brett started crying, and Paige just stared silently at him. She was a teenager now, and I suspected she knew at least some of what had been going on between Bob and me.

I started to add something, but Bob jumped in. "We are getting a divorce," he said, "but I'm going to tell you right now that it is not your mother's fault. It's *my* fault." He didn't elaborate. He didn't have to.

Now I was the one staring at Bob. After all the lying, the gaslighting, the relentless cruelty of the past thirty years, *now* he was finally owning up to what he'd done? I couldn't believe it.

And do you know what I did? For half a second, I actually thought, *Oh, maybe he's starting to come around. Maybe he really can change.* I mean, that was almost all it took to reel me back in—just one simple gesture of honesty. But then—thank god—another, louder voice cut in. *Oh no, Sheila*, this one said. *Don't even go there.*

I was grateful to Bob for admitting to the kids that the failure of our marriage was his fault. I had never expected him to, and I was surprised when he did. But it was far too little, far too late. Now I just had to put one foot in front of the other until we got to the other side of the divorce. It still wouldn't be easy, but at least it seemed like he wasn't going to fight me.

After that conversation, Paige, Brett, and I moved out to Salamander Farm full-time. They had been going to school at Sidwell Friends— where Debra Lee's son also was a student, awkwardly enough—but now I enrolled them at the Hill School in Middleburg. I was incredibly relieved to be out of DC, away from the prying eyes and gossiping tongues and everyday cruelties of people there, but I still left some of my clothes in our house, because the vagaries of divorce law meant that I could lose some of the settlement if I moved out completely before the divorce was finalized. As of that point, I still hadn't even filed yet.

Bob's uncharacteristic burst of honesty didn't last. One afternoon, he drove out to the farm to talk through some details, and I made us a nice lunch. We sat out on the back patio, the view of the mountains stretching out before us. And somehow, we got into it all over again about his cheating and his lies. He started up again with the insults and the gaslighting, and I got pissed off.

"Why did you even marry me?" I asked. "You never wanted to be a husband. I don't think you ever even loved me."

He shook his head, then said, "Come on, now, Sheila. Sure I did."

"Take your ring off," I said. He just sat there. "Take it *off*!" I was shouting now, but I didn't care who heard. He pulled the wedding band off his finger, and I grabbed it and threw it as far as I could into the grass. Bob didn't say anything, didn't get up to look for it—he didn't react at all, really. He just kept on eating his lunch, and when he was finished, he got up and left.

As soon as his car was out of the driveway, I went out into the yard. Because predictably enough, even though Bob didn't care about the ring, I felt terrible about having thrown it out there. I poked around in that grass for twenty minutes, even getting down on my hands and knees at one point, but I never could find it. It's still out there, or maybe a deer came and swallowed it, or a bird carried it to her nest. By now, it's probably just buried under a layer of dirt, never to be seen again. A once shiny thing, buried and gone—just like the marriage.

I knew Bob was looking at selling the company, but since I wasn't involved with BET at any level anymore, I didn't know any of the details. I was just hunkering down in Middleburg with my kids, trying to pull myself together to start a new phase of life. Every so often, I'd travel to see my mother in Illinois or go up to New York for a meeting about one of my philanthropic ventures. It was on one of those trips that I learned BET had been sold.

I was walking through Times Square on November 3, 2000, when I glanced up at the big electronic news ticker screen and saw the headline. BET had been bought by Viacom, and the price was—*Hold on, can that be right?*—$2.3 billion. Viacom, led by Sumner Redstone, was paying that amount for the company in a stock swap—and also taking on nearly $600 million in debt. So the actual selling price was nearly $3 billion.

My knees went wobbly. This was an inconceivable number, beyond my wildest imaginings of what the company might sell for. We were carrying a lot of debt, and of course had to pay back John Malone what he had invested, so it wasn't like Bob and I would personally walk away with that amount. But even taking that into account, this would be a truly incredible payday for the risks we had taken and all those years of work. I stood there staring at the screen long after it had flashed to other stories, unable to believe what my eyes had just seen.

When all the accounts were settled, Bob and I would end up with $1.4 billion in shared stock. And based on the few conversations we'd had about an eventual divorce settlement, I knew his intention was to split our assets down the middle. For all the worrying I had done about whether leaving Bob would decimate me financially, the sale of BET meant that I would end up in a better position than I could ever have dreamed of. It was like I'd been running the world's longest marathon, but just as my legs were about to give out, I could finally see the finish line.

Not long after the BET sale, I began looking for a divorce attorney. Because of the size of the settlement, and the fact that Bob and I were public figures, I wanted to hire someone with experience in high-profile cases. I made a call to one lawyer who gently turned me down, saying she had a conflict of interest. I found out she was representing Debra Lee in her divorce from Randall Coleman—which of course just made me want to end my own marriage faster. If Debra was divorcing her husband to be with Bob, I wanted to be gone before that happened.

The next call I made was to an attorney named Sandy Ain. A friend of mine had used him in her divorce and recommended him highly, so I set up an appointment. Sandy turned out to be a lovely person, very calm and deliberate. He started out with a few questions, including why I wanted to divorce Bob. I said, "Because he's having an affair with Debra Lee."

To my surprise, Sandy nodded. "Yes, he is," he said. I couldn't believe it. It was hard enough knowing that everyone at BET was talking about the affair, but apparently the whole of Washington, DC, was in on the discussion.

"Well, who *doesn't* know about this?" I asked Sandy, frustrated.

"Everyone knows about it, Sheila," he said. I felt that familiar stab of shame, but at the same time I appreciated Sandy's honesty.

"I want to get this moving," I told him. "I need to get out of this marriage."

"We'll move on it as soon as possible," he said, "but it's going to take a while."

"No it won't," I said. And I plopped a pile of paperwork onto his desk. It was all the files I had been collecting—all the information about our finances, our assets, our real estate holdings. "This is everything," I told Sandy. "Have a look, and I'll call you tomorrow."

The divorce ended up taking fourteen months, which was slower than I wanted but much faster than a divorce with that many assets to untangle would usually be. Sandy did a magnificent job, and as he told me later, the negotiations with Bob's lawyer were complicated but cordial. Bob didn't push back on anything that I asked for. There were certain assets I wanted, such as Salamander Farm, and he agreed to cede them to me outright. After all those years of treating me so badly, it was as if he finally felt some responsibility to acknowledge what I'd done for him, our family, and our company.

Although I was relieved that the divorce seemed to be moving along smoothly, I was still deep in the woods emotionally. The damage done during more than three decades of marriage to Bob would take a very, very long time to undo. In fact, the two years following the sale of BET, despite providing me peace of mind about my financial situation, would turn out to be some of the worst times of all.

I call those two years my "dark period," because a cloud of depression descended on me. I couldn't find my way out, couldn't figure out who I was. I had gotten together with Bob at age seventeen, which meant that I had never experienced adult life without him. Through all those years of emotional abuse, he had destroyed not only my self-esteem but also my sense of self, period. I didn't know who I was without Bob Johnson, and I wasn't sure how to find out.

I felt incredibly vulnerable, like I had been torn right open. The truth is, even with all his cruelty, I had loved Bob. When you love someone, you open yourself up to them. As miserable as I had been with him, leaving him was still like pulling out a piece of myself, leaving a gaping hole. It was scary, and it was painful. I was sleeping poorly and felt exhausted every day. And even though deep down I knew I was doing the right thing, it was hard not to second-guess myself. Because when the life you've spent decades building suddenly disappears, it is disorienting and frightening.

Forty years earlier, my mother had felt lonely and socially adrift after my father left. I felt the same way now. Everybody knew that Bob had been cheating on me, and when I walked into a room it felt like all eyes turned to me. I knew people were gossiping, because

Washington, DC, is a place that thrives on gossip. And sometimes, rather than whispering behind my back, people would come right up and say things to me, apparently thinking that would be helpful.

"Girl, he really messed you over, didn't he?" someone would say. Or, "You know, I saw Bob and Debra out on Saturday night. They're not even bothering to hide it anymore." Every time someone made a comment like this, it tore the wound right back open again. This was too painful to endure, so I stopped going into DC for events. I resolved to stay in Middleburg as much as I could, to protect myself. But withdrawing from society and isolating myself like that only added to my feelings of loneliness.

I had Brett and Paige, and they brought much-needed light into my life. But any time parents get divorced, no matter the reason, it's hard on the kids. And they had just transferred schools, so that added another layer of change and uncertainty to their lives. I wanted to comfort them, to reassure them that everything would be okay. But I was such a hot mess myself, I wasn't sure I even believed that.

Two of the people who helped me the most during this period were Mary Henderson and my driver, George Walker. They saw me at my worst. And they never wavered in offering care and support for the kids and me. Mary made sure there were meals on the table, and George made sure we all got to wherever we needed to go. He even taught the kids to drive. I continued to talk to Mary and also to Susan Starrett. Just putting one foot in front of the other, trying to get through this depression like you'd cross a rickety bridge over a raging river.

The way my mother had come back to herself after her own period of darkness was by going to the First Baptist Church in Melrose Park. The church has long been the backbone of Black American society, and my mother found strength within its walls. She believed she felt the presence of God, but she also was surrounded by a community of women who supported and cared for her. It brought her back to life.

I'm not a churchgoing person. Never have been. But a woman named Pam Hooker, who was my assistant at BET and then came to work with me in Middleburg, said, "Sheila, maybe you just need to sit back for a while and get with God." She knew I had no plans to attend any organized services, so she invited me to do Bible study with her and her husband. It actually did help me for a while. And then I discovered something I called my "prayer path."

It was a looping trail through the trees on Salamander Farm—almost like a maze, a path where I could walk and walk and never see another soul. In fact, it was far enough away from any other people that I could just scream and cry and never worry about being heard. I had so many emotions roiling within, from sadness to shame to fury. I could let it all out on my prayer path, as if purging a poison from my body.

When you're out of sorts mentally and emotionally, you put yourself in danger physically too. I was a shambling mess in the years after Bob and I split, banging into counters, slamming my fingers in doors, burning myself at the stove. There was a serious disconnect between my body and my soul, and I was constantly ending up with bruises and nicks everywhere, because my mind was wandering. I didn't know how to be present in the moment anymore, and pretty soon the little accidents turned into bigger ones.

One gorgeous autumn day, I decided it would be nice to spend some time horseback riding with Paige. She had become a serious equestrian, with goals of making the national team and going to the Olympics. She rode beautifully, and she loved it so much that I thought it might be nice to try to improve my own riding, to spend more time with her. I wasn't what you'd call a natural rider, but I'd spent enough time on horses to feel reasonably comfortable, and this felt like a way we could bond. I decided to join Paige as she worked with her trainer, Jeff Wirthman, practicing jumps.

I mounted a horse named Warlock and trotted out into the arena. Jeff talked me through how to do a low jump, and after getting all the pointers, I decided to give it a try. Everything was going fine until we got close to the obstacle, when suddenly Warlock spooked. He bucked, kicking his hind legs into the air, and I went flying over his head. I was still holding the reins as I went down, and as soon as I hit the ground, he reared up, lifting his front legs and then crashing his hooves back down hard—right onto my chest.

I heard the awful sound before I felt any pain. It was a thunderous *crunch*, the sound of hundreds of pounds crashing directly onto my rib cage. I was so shocked, I'm not even sure I made a sound. In an instant, six of my ribs broke and my left lung collapsed.

I lay there, unable to breathe, trying to understand what had just happened. Paige started crying, completely freaked out. Jeff immediately called 911, and fortunately the ambulance got there quickly. On the ride to Loudoun Hospital, the EMT kept sticking his hand up my shirt, and although I was in horrific pain, I was alert enough to yell, "Get your hands out of there!" I know he had to check my injuries, but I swear it seemed like he was trying to feel me up.

The doctors kept me in the hospital for about a week. Bob came and visited me one evening, and I was in so much pain and discomfort that day, I was afraid to be alone. I asked him to stay, and he actually did. He slept in the chair in my hospital room—another act of kindness that surprised me. It was as if he could display any sort of emotional connection to me only when he no longer felt bound by marriage vows to do it.

I remember thinking during the ambulance ride, when I wasn't fighting off the EMT's wandering hands, *God, if you just let me live, I will never get on another horse again.* And I never have. I'll never know what caused Warlock to spook, but I couldn't help myself—I stayed mad at him for throwing me. Maybe karma caught up with that horse, because about a year later, he ended up getting—and I'm not making this up—cancer of the penis. Sorry, Warlock.

As serious as my injuries were, I know how lucky I was. If that horse had come down an inch or so farther to the right, his hooves would have crushed my heart and killed me instantly. And the fact that I managed not to land on my head, even as I kept holding the reins, is another miracle. A few weeks after my accident, a woman who lived down the road from us was thrown from her horse too. But unlike me, she broke her neck and was paralyzed, and she died not long after that. Life is sometimes just a matter of inches, and on that day, as bad as the accident was, I came out on the fortunate side.

I spent a few months recovering, and I managed to get back on my prayer path just as the leaves started turning and the winter chill started blowing in across the Shenandoah. One afternoon, a fierce storm coated the farm in a sheet of ice, and Paige said, "I'm going to go check on the horses." I told her I'd come, too, and followed her out the back door.

We have an outdoor stairwell that leads down from the house toward the stables, and as Paige got to the bottom of it, she turned back and yelled, "Mom, be careful! It's really icy." I yelled back, "Okay!" and went to take hold of the railing—and that's when my feet flew out from under me. I bumped down those stone steps like a rag doll, and by the time I reached the bottom, my tibia was broken clean through and my ankle was shattered. Back to the hospital I went, this time for surgery to put screws into my ankle.

Lying in my hospital bed, I called my mother. She still didn't know I had decided to divorce Bob, but it was obvious to her that I was an absolute mess. "Something's not right in your life, Sheila," she said. "You're distracted. You're thinking about other things, when you need to pay attention to what you're doing."

My mother knew as well as anyone that when a woman is at her lowest point, her body gives out on her. She'd experienced that when she collapsed in our kitchen all those years ago. She was worried about me, because in addition to the fact that I was under obvious emotional strain, if I kept on having accidents like this, I was going to do permanent damage to myself.

"You need to sit still," she told me. "Stop running around and just rest. It's time for you to relax and figure out what you need in life."

I promised her I would. And I really did try. But the truth is, I'm not the kind of person who can sit still for long. So as much as I wanted to spend some time in quiet contemplation, and as sincere as my intentions were to slow down, they went right out the window on my next drive down Washington Street, the main road in Middleburg. Because that's when I finally, after dozens of times driving past it, got fed up with seeing a certain flag hanging at the entrance to my town.

As a toddler with my father, mother, and brother, G. P. *Author's archives.*

Playing with my brother in his crib at our house in Monessen, Pennsylvania. We moved thirteen times before I turned ten. *Author's archives.*

In elementary school. Light-skinned like my father, I passed as white in second grade. *Author's archives.*

Go Pirates! Filled with school spirit at Proviso East High School in Chicago. *Author's archives.*

Cheerleaders Work to Generate Enthusiasm

Despite unpredictable performances by the Illinois football team,
a determined Illini cheerleading
squad proved that spirit still existed
at Zuppke Field. In trying to keep
up this spirit, the squad renovated
many of their traditional programs
and initiated several new cheering
techniques. One new highlight of
the football season was snappy flag
routines, synchronized to the quick
moving marches of the band. Flashy
pom pom routines further empha-
sized their bouncy, spirited pace.
Pyramid formations and acrobatics
were two more important techniques
which displayed their agility. The
new "mini tramp" aided the squad
in executing their gymnastic skills.

With the basketball season, spirit
was still the key, although not as
hard to excite. For the first time in
several years, male members of the
squad cheered at the basketball
games. The squad was able to rotate
different cheerleaders in the upper
block. As a result, more sideline
cheers were started by fans in the
upper sections.

Sheila Crump produces a big smile for the conquests of her gridiron heroes.

In the late 1960s, I became the first Black cheerleader at the University of Illinois. The Illio.

Sheila Crump Named Soloist for Concert

$1; student tickets at 50 cents.

Sheila was chosen for this honor through competitive audition held recently at both schools. Sheila will play Haydn's Concerto in G Major for Violin and String Orchestra. The string orchestra will be made up of predominantly upper classmen of the township orchestra.

"During Sheila's four years as a student at Proviso East," states Miss Susan Sterrett, director of orchestras for the Proviso high schools, "she has established herself as a fine worker and competitor and has brought honors to herself and her school." The violin was a project started in grade school and has become an object of increasing interest during the past few years.

She has been a member of the Proviso East high school orchestra for four years, serving as its president and concertmistress for two years.

Sheila held the same position of leadership for 2 years in the Proviso Township orchestra, made up of the best students of both East and West high schools, and last year was named the "Outstanding String Member of the Orchestra."

In January of 1966, she won a position in the Illinois All-State festival orchestra, along with four other Proviso orchestra students, as a result of her performance in the district orchestra. She was then named concertmistress, or first chair violin player, of the 1966 Illinois All-State Orchestra in Peoria, the most coveted honor for a high school violinist.

In addition to her musical ability, Sheila has for three years been a member of the Proviso East cheerleading squad and served as captain for the 1965-66 school year. During her sophomore year she was voted a National Cheerleading champion at the Michigan State University summer camp for cheerleaders.

The HERALD

SHEILA CRUMP, Maywood, is the featured soloist for the spring concert of the Proviso Township High Schools orchestras, to be held Sunday, April 24, at 3:15 p.m. in the Proviso East auditorium.

The concert is open to the public and adult tickets may be purchased at the door for

I fell in love with the violin as a child. By my senior year of high school, I was first chair All-State.

The Daily Herald.

When I pick up a violin, it feels like a part of me.

Author's archives.

With my high school music
teacher and mentor,
Susan Starrett

Author's archives.

Susan and I
have become
lifelong friends,
staying close
for more than
five decades.

Author's archives.

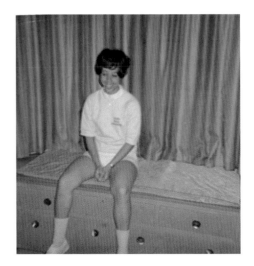

My first week at college. Just seventeen, I met an older student named Robert Johnson at orientation. Two years later, we married.

Author's archives.

After college, I grew my hair out and started dressing in '70s style.

Author's archives.

While teaching music at Sidwell Friends School, I got a side gig acting in a play. I met someone there who'd come back into my life in a surprising way years later.

The Washington Star.

Bette Howard, the director of "Ceremonies in Dark Old Men," gives some advice to theater newcomer, Sheila Johnson, who is a music teacher at Sidwell Friends School.

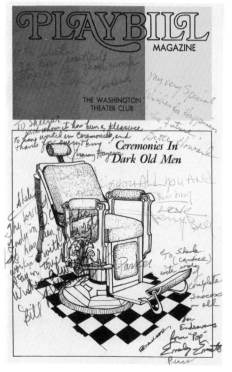

My Playbill for *Ceremonies in Dark Old Men*, signed by fellow actors

Author's archives.

Queen Noor took a special interest in my orchestra,
giving my students the opportunity of a lifetime—
to play in Jordan. *Author's archives.*

With my students at the Jerash Festival, outside Amman *Author's archives.*

We started
BET in
1979, with
a $15,000
loan and a
great idea.
Author's archives.

My cofounder
at BET,
Bob Johnson
Author's archives.

After selling BET and divorcing Bob, I started to find my feet again by getting involved with CARE. Here, I'm in Tanzania with local women and then– CARE president and CEO, Helene Gayle. © *CARE.*

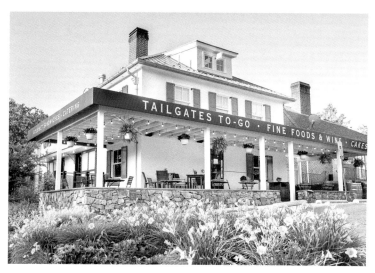

Market Salamander, my first venture in Middleburg, also helped pull me out of a dark place. *Author's archives.*

Marrying Bill Newman in 2005,
one of the happiest days of my life. *Author's archives.*

I love this photo of Bill—
who actually is a really good cook!

Author's archives.

With my dearest friend Della Britton, head of the Jackie Robinson Foundation; Jackie's widow, the activist Rachel Robinson; and Len Coleman. Selling BET enabled me to get seriously involved with philanthropic causes. *The Jackie Robinson Foundation.*

At a Parsons School of Design benefit, with New School president Bob Kerrey, President Bill Clinton, and my husband Bill. I was fortunate enough to serve many years on the Parsons board. *Getty Images.*

The official opening of Salamander Resort & Spa in 2013–a day I feared would never come. From left to right: David Gergen, Scott York, Middleburg Mayor Betsy Davis, my son, Brett, me, Prem Devadas, Rita McClenny, and Giardy Ritz. *Robert T. Williams.*

Aerial view of my beloved resort,
nestled at the foot of the Bull Run Mountains

Jim Hanna.

With my mother
at the Salamander
opening. "Sheila,"
she said to me, "I
am not dying until
the doors of that
resort open." She
died two months
after it opened.

Author's archives.

My beautiful mother,
my rock. I miss her still.

Author's archives.

With my children, Paige and Brett. I am so proud of them. *Author's archives.*

The Family Reunion, our celebration of African American cuisine and culture, is one of my favorite events at Salamander. Here I am with Salamander president Prem Devadas and our amazing chef and creator of the event, Kwame Onwuachi.

Author's archives.

With my longtime chief of staff, Giardy Ritz. I have the best team in the business.

Author's archives.

Rocking out with songwriter Diane Warren at the
Middleburg Film Festival, another of my favorite events. *Joy Asico.*

Celebrating the Washington Mystics championship in 2019.
These truly are the best years of my life. *Getty Images.*

Ten

FREE

Every time I drove into Middleburg, I'd pass by the Powder Horn Gun & Antique shop at the entrance to town. I didn't mind that; this is Virginia hunt country, so guns are a part of life out here. But what I did mind was how the owner had decorated the place—with a giant Confederate flag hanging in the window.

I hated seeing that thing. Even just a glimpse of it was enough to put me in a bad mood for the rest of the day. And there was no way to avoid it, as the shop sat right on Washington Street, the main road running through Middleburg.

But what could I do? A gun shop owner in rural Virginia wasn't going to jump right to it if a Black woman walked in and told him to take down that hateful piece of cloth. At first, I figured I'd have to get used to it. Yet as the weeks rolled by, I just could not. Every time I passed it, even making a point of looking the other way, I could feel my heartbeat start pounding in my ears. I had grown to love Middleburg, but I just couldn't stand seeing that flag every time I drove into town.

And then . . . I had an idea. I called Sandy Ain. "There's a piece of real estate on Washington Street I'm interested in. I want you to find out confidentially how I can buy the building."

"Okay," he said. "What do you want it for?"

"Because there's a Confederate flag hanging in the window," I said. "And I am just damn tired of looking at it."

As my real estate agent had said a few years back, anything's for sale if you can convince someone to sell it. We made a good offer to the owner of 200 West Washington Street, and soon enough the building was mine. He packed up his flag and closed down his gun shop, now with plenty of money to retire on, and I made plans to open a beautiful, welcoming café and market. I decided to name it Market Salamander. And although it didn't open until 2004, I trace the beginning of my recovery to the moment I realized I could buy that building and create something lovely there.

That was the moment I realized that I could do some good here in Middleburg—to help revive a dying town and, in doing so, hopefully revive myself too.

In 2000, the year I moved out to Salamander Farm full-time, Middleburg felt like a gorgeous but slightly shabby relic of a bygone age. Founded in the eighteenth century as "Chinn's Crossroads," it was home to only about seven hundred people, more like a village than a town. The main street was lined with modest shops and a few restaurants, and many of the storefronts were boarded up. The historic centerpiece was the Red Fox Inn & Tavern, established in 1728 and known as one of the oldest continuously operating inns in the United States. But apart from that, the town felt as dead as a doornail.

Middleburg was, and still is, surrounded by horse country, including sprawling estates owned by some of the wealthiest people in the Washington area. Abe Pollin, the owner of several Washington sports teams, had a farm right near mine, and Washington Redskins owner Jack Kent Cooke owned another not too far away before his death in 1997. Jackie Mars, the heiress to the Mars candy fortune, lives in the next town over. And actor Robert Duvall, who's a big horse aficionado, lives with his wife, Luciana Pedraza, on a nearby estate called Byrnley Farm. Yet for all the wealth represented in these surrounding estates, many were outside of Middleburg itself, so it wasn't as if the town had tons of tax revenue flowing in. It was financially strapped, struggling to keep its stores open and its roads paved.

Culturally, Middleburg was white, southern, conservative, and not particularly open to change. And yet, the locals were very welcoming when I moved to the area with Brett and Paige. Neighbors brought by jars of homemade jam and fresh-baked loaves of bread, and people in those little shops and restaurants were always friendly. Still, running underneath all that southern hospitality were occasional flashes of racist attitude. I was obviously not part of the area's usual demographic, so when I moved to town and embraced horse-country culture, some people weren't quite sure what to make of that.

Not long after we bought Salamander Farm, Billy Moroney and another local trainer, Chuck Keller, approached me about hosting the Orange County hunt.

"Host the what, now?" I asked. I hadn't heard of it, so Billy explained. The Orange County Hounds was a hundred-year-old fox-hunting club. The members would dress in traditional attire—dark or scarlet jackets, white breeches, and knee-high black boots—then ride horses out into the countryside with a pack of specially bred hounds to chase foxes. There were many other rituals associated with hunt days, too, including a traditional big breakfast and ceremonial glasses of brandy.

Well, that all sounded like fun to me, so I told Billy I'd love to host. I hired a catering company and waiters, set up some tables, and rented some gorgeous silver trays and big brandy snifters, and on the appointed day, the members of the hunt came out to Salamander Farm. The scene that day was like something out of *Downton Abbey*, a gorgeous slice of traditional English country life right in my own backyard. And I had made sure everything was prepared according to tradition, with plenty of eggs, crisp bacon, potatoes, and french toast—the works.

Just as everyone was settling in for breakfast, which we served in the indoor riding arena, one man just couldn't help himself. He turned to the guy next to him and said, "Well, I guess we'll be having chitlins today." I suppose he thought he was being funny. But what he didn't realize was that I was standing close enough to hear. I strode up to him and said, "You know, I don't eat chitlins. But if you want some, I can ask the caterer to whip some up for you." He turned bright red and apologized, and I just smiled sweetly and walked away.

That's when I ran into two Black women I had hired for the event. They were both locals, older women who had lived for decades in these rolling hills. And they were smiling so big, just enjoying the hell out of themselves. "Honey," one of them said to me as she gestured toward the dozens of white men milling about in their red coats, "never in my *lifetime* did I think I'd see all these white folks enjoying themselves in a Black-owned house." We laughed, and then she said, "This is history!"

I hadn't expected to fall in love with this area, but there was something about it that just felt like home. I can't explain why a Black violin player from Maywood, Illinois, feels so comfortable in rural Virginia, the heart of the Confederacy. And as a person who got six ribs crushed by a horse, it makes absolutely no sense that I still love everything having to do with the equestrian life. Yet somehow, Middleburg became the place where my soul feels most at ease. I didn't just want to be someone who bought a pretty piece of land and sat on it, twiddling her thumbs, though. I wanted to truly become part of the Middleburg community.

Fortunately, the fact that my kids were in school there, combined with my financial position, provided me a perfect way to start giving to the community. I knew how incredibly fortunate I was after the BET sale went down, and I wanted to share that windfall with the people and institutions in my new hometown.

As soon as Paige and Brett were enrolled at Hill School, I joined the board and made a donation to build a new music room. The school had a strings program—and to my delight, their curriculum included the textbooks I'd helped Paul Rolland write all those years ago. But those budding young musicians deserved more. I was excited to provide a proper music room for their studies—one with great acoustics and storage space for instruments.

The Hill School itself was gorgeous, a quaint collection of buildings on 140 acres of lush green land just south of Washington Street. A devoted staff of teachers served about two hundred students, and among their extracurriculars was a strong theater program, headed by a brilliant educator named Tom Sweitzer. But I had noticed that the kids didn't have a dedicated space for their plays, and they had to store costumes and props in other buildings scattered across the campus. So, after making the donation for the music room, I had another idea.

One afternoon, I cornered the school's headmaster, Tom Northrup, at a horse show. "I need to talk to you about something," I said. Seeing my serious expression, he frowned and asked me what was going on.

"How would you like a dedicated performing arts center?" I asked him.

His eyebrows shot up. "Sheila, are you kidding me?" he asked. I just smiled, and he said, "Oh my goodness, *yes!*"

I told him I wanted to build a performing arts center from the ground up, with smaller stages where the younger students could perform and a larger stage for the bigger shows. It wouldn't be anything ostentatious or fancy, as I wanted it to fit in with the school's existing traditional stone-and-wood architecture. I thought Tom was going to do backflips, he was so happy. We drew up the plans, hired the construction company, and got the building completed within a year.

On September 21, 2002, Tom led a ceremony dedicating the new Sheila C. Johnson Performing Arts Center on the Hill School campus. I'm proud of that building and thrilled to have provided a venue for young people to pursue their love of the arts. It's a warm and welcoming space, the kind of place where memories are made, not only for students and their teachers, but also for the family and friends who come see the performances.

My favorite detail, though, is the framed dedication page mounted inside the front door. It displays the opening date and describes my goal of providing "a venue for children and adults to develop confidence, competence and self-knowledge through experiences on and behind the stage." This encapsulates everything I hope the center can do for young people who find themselves falling in love with the arts—just as I did as a young girl in Maywood, Illinois.

And at the top of the page, there's a photograph of me as a teenager with the woman who taught me all those things and more, Susan Starrett.

I'm fortunate enough never to have been addicted to drugs, alcohol, gambling, or any other kind of vice. But I have to admit that once I started giving away money, I did get a bit addicted to that.

In those first years after the BET sale, I gave $7 million for a new design center to the Parsons School of Design, whose board I had recently joined. I underwrote fundraising galas for the Loudoun Hospital Center and the Piedmont Environmental Council, and gave $100,000 to the Windy Hill Foundation to help build affordable housing in Middleburg. I even raffled off a Mercedes roadster that Bob had given Paige for her sixteenth birthday, because that car was just too fast for a teenager to be driving.

After thirty-three years of always looking to Bob before making a financial move, I was finally free to do whatever I wanted. I didn't have to ask anybody's permission but could just follow my own instincts, wherever they led me. And in early 2002, they led me in a direction I hadn't expected—one that would change my life forever.

I got a call from a real estate broker about a big parcel of land north of Washington Street. "I have three hundred forty acres just outside the town limits," he told me. "It's from Pamela Harriman's estate, and it's spectacular."

Pamela Harriman had been a force of nature in American politics. She was a big fundraiser for Democrats and served as US ambassador to France from 1993 until her death in Paris in 1997. She had been married to Winston Churchill's son, Randolph, then later to the former New York governor Averell Harriman. The Harrimans had owned hundreds of acres of land out in Virginia horse country, and by 2002, much of it had been sold. The parcel of land this broker was calling about was the last one to be put up for sale.

Because the estate was so close to the town of Middleburg, the local people were very nervous about who might buy it and what they might do with it. If it went to a developer, those pristine acres could end up covered with tract houses, destroying the character of the land. Or it could be turned into a boxy chain hotel, an eyesore looming just a few blocks from Washington Street. Middleburg was at a crossroads. It needed some sort of development, because the town lacked an economic engine and needed a new source of revenue. On the other hand, nobody wanted the character of the town and the land to change.

This was a fine line to tread, and I wasn't sure I wanted to be anywhere near it. But when I went to have a look at the property, I was blown away. It was a stunning piece of land, with horse trails running through acres of woods, vast green fields, sparkling creeks, and white-tailed deer bounding among the trees. Standing on the grassy hillside, I could see right down into town, which was close enough to walk to. My heart swelled, and at that moment, the thought popped into my head: *This would be the perfect place for a resort.*

Now, I had never owned a resort. I had never been in the hospitality industry at all. It's not like I had dreamed of doing this my whole life and was just looking for the opportunity to make it happen. All I can say is, there was something transformative about standing there, breathing in the fresh smell of the woods, and suddenly seeing the possibilities inherent in that magical landscape. I realized that I had the power and the opportunity to build something beautiful—a place that would welcome people from all over, help this town I loved, and help me become the author again of my own destiny.

I had no idea what any of the details would look like and no idea how it would all unfold. But I knew I needed that piece of land. I offered $7 million for the parcel, with a thirty-day cash settlement, and I pledged to put half of it under conservation easement, which meant that the land would be protected in its natural state. People in town were ecstatic—particularly the Piedmont Environmental Council, which had been very vocal about not wanting the land to go to a developer.

From the start, I suggested it would be a good place to build a small inn, a decision that initially didn't cause too many ripples. Later, when I decided to expand the plans and build a larger resort, I would face the fight of a lifetime. But for now, everybody was happy, and I felt filled with a new energy—the energy of creating.

Shortly after closing on the purchase, I took some friends for a hike on the land. We pulled on our jackets and boots and set out on a crisp March afternoon to explore. We walked and walked, marveling at the sunlight dappling through the trees, the brambles and thickets where chipmunks played, the white-tailed deer that scattered like ghosts when they heard our approaching footsteps. I couldn't believe all this land was now mine. I couldn't believe how *much* of it there was. And then . . . I couldn't figure out where the hell we were. We had hiked so deep into the 340 acres, none of us knew how to find our way out.

We kept hiking and hiking, looking up through the trees to try to see which way the sun was setting. We were all laughing about the fact that we were lost, but after a while the laughter turned to nervous chuckles and then silence. My god, which way was out? It was a chilly day, but by the time we finally reached a clearing and figured out where we were, we were all dripping with sweat. My heart was pounding with relief. We had made it!

Little did I know, but this day was a microcosm of what was to come. It would take more than a decade to create the resort, and that journey would involve more twists and turns, fear and heartbreak, than I ever expected was possible. And it was all starting right now.

In August 2002, I took Paige and Brett up to Long Island, New York, for the Hampton Classic Horse Show. At age sixteen, Paige was at the top of her riding game, and she would be taking part in the competition. Brett and I were there to cheer her on, and Bob was coming up, too, though with our divorce proceedings in their final weeks, I had no plans to spend any time with him. I just wanted to focus on my kids and have a good time at the show.

At one point, Brett and I walked into the concourse area to get something to eat. That's when a young Black man walked up to me and said, "Hello, Mrs. Johnson. Do you have a minute to talk?"

I didn't know the guy, but he obviously knew who I was, so I nodded. He introduced himself as Brett Pulley, the *Forbes* writer who had covered BET for the magazine. I don't remember what he asked me first, but I do remember that very quickly after we started speaking, he said something like, "When did you know about Bob and Debra's affair?"

My heart dropped into my stomach. *What the hell?* I'm standing here with my twelve-year-old son, minding my own business, and a total stranger comes up in public to ask me *that*? I just stared at him for a second, my face getting hot and tears welling up. Then, before I realized what I was doing, I opened my mouth and started talking.

I don't remember exactly what I said, but I can tell you what Brett Pulley reported in the book he later published, *The Billion Dollar BET*. Because as it turned out, Pulley was there at the Hampton Classic not to watch horses, but to do research on Bob and me. Bob had actually warned his family members about the upcoming book, and he had told them not to talk to Pulley. But I was taken by surprise, and a little bit in shock, and before I knew it, I was blurting out answers to his questions.

Here's what Pulley wrote about our brief conversation:

"There is a sadness in me," Sheila confides during an interview with me that same day. "I just feel so bad. But I have to go on with my life." . . .

She still praises her soon-to-be ex-husband. "He's a brilliant businessman," she says. "And there will be a part of me that will always love him." But, she reveals, extramarital affairs "were his biggest problem. He has got a body count."

Bob's relationship with Debra Lee, whom Sheila had been so close to over the years, has left her stunned. "That affair with Debra just hurt me more than anything, because I knew her, and I couldn't believe she would do that," Sheila says. "There was obviously a side of her I never knew . . . I find the whole thing tragic."

It was definitely not my habit to talk to reporters about any of this, but Pulley had caught me off guard. We spoke briefly, and then

I tried to gesture subtly to my son, who was standing nearby. I didn't want to get into everything, especially with twelve-year-old Brett right there. But Pulley had gotten what he needed, and within the next two years, my quotes would come out not only in his book, but in the *Washington Post*'s gossip column, "The Reliable Source."

The *Post* just seemed to love poking this particular bruise. The column's headline read, "The Ex-Spouse Who Roared," and reporter Richard Lei wrote breathlessly that I had been "willing to dish" about Bob's "philandering." He made the whole thing sound like a game, which upset not only me but also Brett and Paige. In fact, the morning the column came out, Brett was at a friend's house following a sleepover. His friend's dad shoved the paper at him over the breakfast table and asked, "How dare your mother talk about your father like this?" Brett was left feeling embarrassed and angry.

All of that was in the future, though. For the moment, I just wanted to get away from Brett Pulley and watch my daughter compete in the Hampton Classic. Bob was sitting in the bleachers several rows up, and I couldn't even look at him. Our divorce proceedings had been going on for more than a year, and I was just desperate to have them finished. I had taken my first baby steps toward reclaiming my life, but I needed to be officially divorced from him to be truly free.

On September 18, 2002, I walked into the Arlington Circuit Court building for the divorce hearing. This was it, the final step in the dissolution of my thirty-three-year marriage to Robert Johnson. I was flooded with emotions that morning, a jumbled mess of feelings ranging from excitement and happiness to sorrow and grief for what the kids and I had been through. But mostly what I felt was relief.

Through our lawyers and a mediator, Bob and I had agreed, without any real conflict, on what was essentially a fifty-fifty split of our assets. In fact, everything was so settled that he didn't even bother showing up for this hearing, nor did he send a lawyer. Sandy Ain and I walked into the courtroom together, and when I looked at the judge who was presiding, a heavyset Black man with a trim, graying beard, I had to do a double take.

"Hey, Sandy," I whispered. "I think I know that judge."

Sandy's eyebrows shot up. "How do you know him?" he asked. Because this was, for obvious reasons, not a great time to have a conflict of interest.

"I mean, I haven't seen him in years," I said. "We were in a play together back in the seventies."

That's right. The judge was none other than Bill Newman, my fellow DC actor whom I'd enjoyed talking with so much back when we were performing in *Ceremonies in Dark Old Men* together in 1973. I couldn't believe it. I'd had no idea what had happened to Bill after the play closed down, as we didn't keep in touch. I'd assumed he'd kept acting, because he was really good at it, but he'd obviously gone to law school and taken a different path in life altogether. And now here he was, presiding over my divorce hearing. What were the chances?

Sandy said, "Don't say a word. Let's just get through the proceeding, and then you can go up and speak to him if you want."

The hearing took very little time, as everything was settled and the paperwork was ready. Honestly, Judge Newman didn't have to do much of anything—just ask a few questions and sign the divorce decree at the end. Once that was finished, I looked at him and said, "Your Honor, may I approach the bench?"

"Yes, you may," he replied in a smooth baritone that I remembered well.

I walked up to where he sat, smiled, and said, "By any chance, do you remember me?" Nearly thirty years had passed since we had seen each other, so I wasn't making any assumptions.

The judge kept his eyes down on the paperwork. "Oh, yes I do," he said. Then I thought I saw a hint of a smile on his face too. And then finally, he looked up. "It's good to see you, Sheila."

"You're a judge now!" I said, and he chuckled. He told me he'd continued acting for a while but then decided to go to law school.

"Growing up around here, I always figured that if nothing else, I could always go to law school," he said, "because everybody is a lawyer here."

The two of us chatted for a little bit, just getting caught up like old friends do, and I found myself remembering how comfortable I always felt with him. I looked at his left hand and didn't see a ring, which surprised me, and I wondered for a brief moment—was he gay? I couldn't figure why he wouldn't be married, as he was a kind, good-looking, successful, stable man. Whatever was going on, I enjoyed our little catch-up so much, I said, "You know, we should have lunch together one of these days." He just nodded and said, "You know where to find me." He probably didn't think I meant it—but I did.

Later on, I would find out that Bill wasn't even supposed to preside over my hearing that day. Another judge had been on the docket, but for some reason he couldn't make it that morning, so the day before, Bill was tapped to fill in. We had requested an earlier start time to the hearing, so we could get in and out of there without drawing any notice, and Bill told me his first thought was, *Who the hell are these people? Judges take the bench when they take the bench.* Then he'd looked at the paperwork and realized whose case it was. Just as I had done with Sandy, he'd checked with others to make sure there was no possible conflict if he presided over my hearing. He and I hadn't spoken in thirty years, and he'd spoken to Bob only once since then, in a strange exchange in New Orleans about five years earlier. I would hear about that later on—after Bill and I started dating.

I walked out of the courtroom that day with a spring in my step and a big smile on my face. Now that the divorce was official, I could finally tell my mother what was going on. Standing at the top of the courthouse steps, I called her.

"Mom," I shouted into my cell phone, "guess what just happened!"

"What?!" she asked.

"I just got divorced!"

And she shouted right back: "Praise the Lord!" Then we laughed until the tears came out, savoring the moment together—two women who had been through hell, who knew what it was like to fight to hold a family together, who had felt rage and anxiety and fear, and who had both, somehow, someway, made it out the other side.

And if that wasn't enough to propel me forward into the next act of my life, there was one more incident a month later that definitively marked this as the end of an era.

On October 26, 2002, my father, Dr. George P. Crump Sr., died at age eighty-four in Mobile, Alabama. I found out from my brother,

G. P., who called me to ask if I planned to go to the funeral. "Absolutely not," I told him. Why would I want to go pay respects in death to a man who'd shown zero respect for me, my mother, or my brother in life?

My father also showed no respect for Brett and Paige, his grandchildren. Though I had never spoken to him again after that day in my uncle's hospital room, my mother somehow ended up back in touch with him later in life. She told me that she once said to him, "You should really get to know Sheila's kids." To which he replied: "They're not mine. So why should I bother?"

They're not mine. The cruelty of this is enough to shatter your heart. My father was referring to the fact that Paige and Brett are adopted, so they're not blood relatives of his. But he knew full well that my mother was also adopted—or rather, she was a foster child who had incorrectly thought she was adopted. He knew the insecurity and anxiety she'd suffered because of it. And even so, he straight-up said those cutting words to her about my children.

I had no interest in saying goodbye to him. I'd done that a long time ago. But my brother wanted to go to the funeral, so he got in touch with my father's widow, the nurse he'd run away with. And what do you think her answer was? She told him she'd rather he didn't come. Irritated and hurt, G. P. went down to Alabama anyway, and he snuck into the funeral home and took a grainy photo of our father in his casket, I suppose to prove that he was actually dead.

Within the span of a month, my divorce was final and my father was gone. It would take me years to heal and a lot of work to find myself again, but for the first time in a long time—maybe ever—I was truly free.

Eleven

BECOMING THE SALAMANDER

Although my conversation with Bill Newman had been short, I'd really enjoyed reconnecting with him. I wanted to see him again, and a couple of weeks after the divorce hearing, the perfect opportunity presented itself. As president of the Washington International Horse Show, I had planned a big fundraising gala at the MCI Center in DC's Chinatown neighborhood. I decided to invite Bill.

I had the envelope addressed to "the Honorable William T. Newman Jr. and Guest." Bill happened to see his mother the day the invitation arrived, so he mentioned it to her. "You remember that young lady I was in *Ceremonies* with, Sheila Johnson?" he said. "I just did her divorce hearing, and now she's inviting me to a party." When he told his mother that he planned to bring along a woman he'd just started seeing, she shook her head.

"No, Bill," she told him. "You go to that party alone. Don't take anybody else." Bill asked her why. "Because I remember how much you liked Sheila back then! You were always talking about her."

Bill laughed. "Mom, she just got a divorce," he said. "I don't think she's necessarily interested in trying to meet someone new." But he decided to follow his mother's advice anyway.

I had planned every detail of that gala and couldn't wait for the night to come—and having Bill there would be icing on the cake. We had invited three hundred guests from all over, including horse-country people like Jackie Mars, and DC movers and shakers. Bob came, too, though I can't remember if I invited him or if he just showed up in support of Paige, who was competing in the show. I sang the national anthem to start the party—the kind of thing that Bob would have rolled his eyes over but I thoroughly enjoyed doing. And during the party, I just had a ball, walking around and chatting with everyone.

After a while, I saw Bill. He was standing by himself, leaning up against one of the bars. I thought he looked like Mr. Cool over there, but as he'd later tell me, he'd just had arthroscopic knee surgery and didn't want to bring the cane he'd been using to get around. So he'd popped a few ibuprofen, hobbled in, and leaned against the bar all night to hide the fact that his knee was killing him.

"Hey, Bill!" I said. "I'm so glad you came." We chatted a little bit about the horse show, and about Paige's riding career and the upcoming competition. As people walked by, I would introduce them to him, but then after a while, he and I just focused on each other, catching up on all that had happened in the decades since we'd been in the play together.

"You know," I told him, "when I walked into that courtroom, I didn't realize it was you at first."

He said, "Well, you know, I've put on a little weight," and then he laughed. "Even though I live alone, I love to cook."

"Why didn't you ever marry?" I asked him. I had been thinking about this question and just couldn't figure it out. Bill was such a lovely man, and I was sure he'd had no trouble attracting women. Was there something about him I needed to know? I figured it made sense just to ask the question rather than standing there wondering.

He smiled. "Don't get me wrong, I've had my share of girlfriends." Now I was the one laughing. "But I just never found the right person." He told me that he'd been on the bench for about fifteen years, and that he'd been a trial lawyer before that. He said he hadn't acted in quite a while but added, "I still love the theater."

"Well, you've certainly done well for yourself," I said. "I always wondered what happened to you, but I never imagined you would have become a judge."

"And you've done pretty well too," he said. "I've kept up with you all these years." It was funny to think about Bill reading about Bob and me in the *Washington Post* or *Washingtonian* magazine. But suddenly all of that seemed very far in the past. Right now, it was just Bill and me, and it felt like we were the only two people in the room.

The next thing we knew, the party was winding down. "Sheila, I've had a really nice time talking with you tonight," Bill said. "I'd love to see you again." I hoped he meant it, because I felt the same way. Sure enough, the next night, he called me. I asked him if he wanted to join me at a friend's birthday party, and that's when he realized he needed to step up his game. He invited me to dinner and to see a production of *Ma Rainey's Black Bottom* at Arena Stage.

So this was what it was like to be with a man who was comfortable in his own skin, who was kind and generous and knew how to take care of a partner. From that first conversation at the gala, I was smitten with Bill. He was a good man and easy to be around.

About a month into our dating, I came down with a terrible cold, and he made chicken soup from scratch and drove all the way from his home in Arlington to Middleburg to deliver it to me. After all those years of feeling judged and gaslit by my ex-husband, to me being with Bill felt like being wrapped in a warm blanket following an ice storm.

The strange thing was, in the three decades that we both lived in the Washington, DC, area, Bill and I had never once come across each other since 1973. I mean, it's not that big of a town, so that seemed pretty incredible to me. But Bill had actually seen Bob a couple of times—including, he told me, in New Orleans during the 1997 Super Bowl weekend.

One of Bill's friends had invited him to a celebrity-filled party, and Bill didn't expect to know anyone there. But when he walked in, he happened to see Bob talking with Denzel Washington. "Hey, I know that guy!" he told his friend, then walked over to say hello. "Hi, Bob," he said. "You don't remember me, but I'm Bill Newman. I did a play with Sheila years ago in DC." At that time, of course, I was still married to Bob, so this was a perfectly reasonable conversation to strike up. But Bob just looked at Bill with disgust. "Man, get out of my face. I don't know you," he said, and pointedly turned away.

Bill was confused, and Denzel seemed embarrassed, even apologizing for Bob's behavior. A little later during the party, though, it became clear why Bob had acted so hostile at the sound of my name. Bill saw him all wrapped up with a light-skinned woman whom he didn't recognize; all he knew for sure was that she wasn't me. I don't know who that woman was, either. Maybe it was Debra Lee, maybe it wasn't. Either way, it was just like Bob to be hanging all over another woman in a public place and not give a rat's ass who saw him doing it.

When Bill told me that story over dinner one night, he leaned in close. "Sheila, I know what you've gone through," he said. "And I want you to know I'm here for you. Whatever you need to do to get past all that."

And that's the moment I fell in love with Bill Newman.

My mother had told me to sit still for a bit, but even though I knew it was good advice, I'm just not built that way. For years, I had been "the wife of Bob Johnson"—never just Sheila Johnson, in my own right. Even though we had started and built BET together, Bob was always and forever the face of it. And despite how relentlessly Bob had belittled my abilities, I knew I was capable of creating and growing businesses on my own. While it might have been better to give myself time to heal before jumping into the next phase of my life, I didn't want to wait. I wanted to get my life back on track, but more than that, I wanted to prove myself.

Right from the start, I ran into all kinds of obstacles. After the divorce was finalized, I needed to move my part of the settlement into my own accounts, then make decisions about how to invest. Bob and I had been with the Bank of New York for a long time, so I asked them for a meeting to discuss everything.

This was a substantial sum of money we were talking about—upward of $800 million—so I expected them to make arrangements for a serious meeting. Instead, they sat me down in a conference room, and a very young woman wearing a twirly skirt came in and started asking me completely irrelevant questions. I couldn't believe it. Without Bob there, they were treating me like a clueless wife rather than a customer in my own right. I kept asking for a higher-level adviser or manager who could help me get my accounts in order, but no one seemed willing to take me seriously.

Eventually, I stood up and said, "I don't like the way I'm being treated here. I'm going to move my money to a different bank." Well, that certainly got their attention. Suddenly, people started scrambling and everybody wanted to make me happy. But I was annoyed—would any man with nearly a billion dollars in the bank have to fight to be taken seriously? Of course not. So, that same week, I withdrew all my funds from Bank of New York and switched to US Trust. Bank of New York kept calling me for days, apologizing and trying to get me to reconsider. I suppose they learned to take women seriously after that.

And that wasn't the only institution that couldn't seem to figure out that women are equal human beings to men. I had trouble setting up an account at the Middleburg bank, as they kept saying I needed Bob's signature—even after our divorce was finalized. I couldn't even get the utility bills for Salamander Farm changed to my name, as they kept wanting Bob's approval as well. "We're *not married anymore!*" I would shout into the phone. "This is *my property!*" Four decades after watching my mother struggle to get a credit card and open a bank account following her divorce, I couldn't believe that I was going through something so similar. I was ready to tear my hair out, until finally I just asked Sandy Ain's office to take care of it all.

This was all part of a big learning curve for me. Even though I was in my fifties, and now a serious philanthropist and investor, I lacked experience in some of the real-world situations that Bob had always handled. I had good business instincts, but if you've never actually hired a full team of employees, chosen high-level consultants for projects, or set up the structure of a new company, there's no way around it: you are going to make mistakes. And I certainly did.

Soon after buying the Harriman land, I started doing a feasibility study about how to build an inn and spa there. I knew what I wanted to create, but there were multiple moving parts to track and coordinate. We had to get permissions from the local governments to build. We had to figure out how to get water, sewage treatment, and electricity to the property. We had to take environmental concerns into account. We had to figure out where, exactly, the structures would be, how they would be designed, and how they would impact the land. This was a huge undertaking, and it would work only if we had the local community's support.

The team that I initially put together didn't pay enough attention to that final point—which was also arguably the most important one. In the beginning, we didn't take enough care with the community leaders, the local councils, and the people in Middleburg who were worried about how a new resort might affect the feel of the town they loved. And unfortunately, I wouldn't realize that we were failing in that task until it was almost too late.

In April 2003, I announced that we would be turning the old Powder Horn gun shop building into a French-style market. I wanted to create a welcoming place—a place where people could come and buy local cheeses and fresh bread and a bottle of wine for a picnic, or prosciutto and fried oysters for a party. We hired Chef Todd Gray of Equinox restaurant in DC to create the menu, and we planned to have café tables so people could buy a sandwich, or an espresso and a pastry, and sit and enjoy themselves. I decided to name the place Market Salamander.

People in town seemed very excited about our plans for the market, just as they had been about the new performing arts center at the Hill School. I felt good about being able to help my new hometown and was excited to create new venues for the community to enjoy. A few months earlier, I had also made a soft announcement about planning a forty-room inn on the Harriman land, and that had also been greeted warmly by most people in town. Everyone still seemed very relieved that the land wouldn't end up being covered with the kind of McMansions that had recently begun sprouting up across Northern Virginia, and I had gained some goodwill with my other projects in town.

Because I had never built an inn or resort before, I sought planning advice from people within that industry. When several of them told me that a forty-room inn wasn't large enough for the site, and that it would be difficult for me to turn a profit, I decided to take their advice and expand the plans for the inn. Instead of forty rooms, we would have fifty-eight, which would slightly increase the footprint of the building but still leave the vast majority of the land untouched.

With our new plan in place, I decided it was time to make an official announcement about our intentions for the Salamander Inn and Spa. On June 19, 2003, we held a groundbreaking on the site. We had a reception under a big white tent, and Chef Todd Gray served crab cakes and roasted corn purée to give a taste of the hospitality I hoped to provide at the inn. Local celebrities showed up, including the *Today* show's Willard Scott, CNN's Bernard Shaw, and even Linda Tripp, who owned a holiday shop in town. But more important, the citizens of Middleburg and local politicians came out in droves to show their support.

Middleburg mayor Tim Dimos spoke, as did the Loudoun County board of supervisors chairman, Scott York. They praised the project to the skies, saying that the Salamander Inn was exactly the kind of development the area needed, as it would preserve most of the land while bringing in visitors and revenue. We displayed drawings of what the rooms would look like, and I gave a short speech about how I hoped the inn would enhance and help the town.

The whole event was so much fun, and the vibe was so positive, that I went home that night feeling better than I had in years. It felt like I was finally crawling out of the dark hole I'd been in since my divorce, and I felt appreciated and embraced in a way that filled my heart. I couldn't believe how fortunate I was to have found a new home in Middleburg, and I couldn't wait to help revive the town. I went to sleep that night feeling a deep contentment with where my life was heading.

The next morning, I was scheduled to fly out of Dulles airport for a short business trip. After breakfast, my driver, George, and I got in the car, and as he pulled out of Salamander Farm's driveway onto Zulla Road, my mouth fell open. Because along both sides were big signs that someone had put up overnight, saying, "Don't BET Middleburg."

Don't BET Middleburg. Now, if someone simply wanted to protest the proposed inn, they could have put up signs saying so. There are a million ways you could phrase that. You could focus on stopping development, or saving the land, or whatever angle you want to take. But "Don't BET Middleburg" is a different kind of message. It's a racially coded way of saying, "You don't belong here." It switches the focus from the inn itself to the race of the person building it. Seeing those signs, I felt stung to my core.

I had figured that some people might oppose the inn. But I'd never imagined they'd come out in the dead of night and put up signs right outside my house. And I certainly never imagined they would launch such an obvious personal attack. I was shocked. And because I was still crawling out of a dark emotional hole, this pushed me right back into it.

Instead of being angry at whoever had put up those signs, my first instinct was to question myself. *Maybe Bob was right*, I thought. *Maybe I'm just no good at anything.* It was as if I could hear his voice in my head, taunting me. *What did you think was going to happen, Sheila? You thought you were all that, but you're not. People don't like you. You are going to fail.*

George kept driving, and I sat in the car, looking out the window at the rolling hills of this deeply Confederate countryside. What *was* I thinking? Did I really believe I could come in here, buy up land, and build my dream resort without any pushback? With my share of the divorce settlement, I could have just gone and lived on an island somewhere, sipping cocktails and watching the sun set. But I had fallen in love with this place. And I truly believed that creating a resort—if done the right way, by integrating it with the surrounding landscape and honoring the culture of the community—would lift up the town.

I was trying to do a *good* thing. And as stung as I felt, I couldn't allow a handful of racist people, who may not even have been from Middleburg, to derail that plan.

That's when I got angry. I called Sandy Ain and said, "We've got a problem." I told him about the signs, and he said he'd make a call to local law enforcement to get them removed. I went ahead with my business trip, knowing that when I got back to Middleburg, I'd have to be prepared to do battle. If people had legitimate questions or concerns about what I was building, I would gladly work with them to resolve the issues. But I would not turn tail and run, no matter how much certain people tried to intimidate me.

And the intimidation tactics, as I would soon find out, had only just begun.

In late July 2003, just a few weeks after the "Don't BET Middleburg" signs went up, the Piedmont Environmental Council took direct aim at my plans for the Salamander Inn and Spa. The PEC had been ecstatic when I bought the Harriman land, and they had loved me when I'd thrown a huge fundraiser for them a year earlier. But now they had decided they didn't like the idea of an inn, so they took out a full-page ad in the *Middleburg Life* newspaper asking, "Is the future of Middleburg a resort town?"

PEC wasn't the only organization that started making noise. The owner of a local real estate company formed a group called Friends of Middleburg, which put up more signs and handed out bumper stickers. People started writing letters to the editors of the local papers, comparing the proposed inn to a McDonald's, while others started referring to it as "Disneyland North." A *Washington Post* reporter named Ian Shapira started poking around Middleburg, getting opinions from both sides. In an August 3 story, he quoted a town council member as saying, "People are concerned she is going over the top . . . We enjoy understated, good taste. We don't want to be glitzy. Sheila would like to spiff us up more than what we're comfortable with." And a cattle farmer was quoted as saying she wanted to create a bumper sticker saying, "Do you want to change the name to Johnsonburg?"

I didn't love all the critical bumper stickers, flyers, signs, and newspaper ads, but most of them were signs of healthy debate. The inn would mark a big change, and I understood why people were nervous about it. And even though some local politicians, including the Middleburg mayor, were in favor of the plan, others felt like we were trying to steamroll the town. Looking back, in that first year and a half, my team didn't take as much care as we should have to make the community feel like we were hearing their concerns.

But none of that excused what happened next.

I was strolling down Washington Street one day with George, on my way to Market Salamander, when I saw an older white man coming toward me. As he passed by, he leaned in close and said, "Black *bitch*." And then he kept walking.

I was too stunned to say anything—but George wasn't. He turned around and walked after the man. "Now, why would you want to say a thing like that?" he demanded. George was a big man, and he towered over the guy, who did look a little intimidated. George stood and watched as the man slunk off, and then he walked me back to the car.

That encounter shook me up, but what upset me more was when people approached my kids. Paige, who was now a teenager, went for a manicure in town one day, and a woman in the shop straight-up started yelling at her. "How *dare* your mother come in here and destroy this beautiful area. Who does she think she is?" The woman said she'd run us all out of town if she had the chance, and Paige got scared. She stepped out onto the sidewalk and called me, upset. "Mom, a woman in the nail salon is coming after me," she said. I told her to find out the woman's name—as it turned out, she was a neighbor of ours—and then I reported it to the police.

We started getting hate mail at Salamander Farm, some of it with death threats. I hired a security team and would just turn the letters over to them. I tried not to think about it, but none of us were sleeping well, afraid of whether people might act on the threats they were making. Maybe I'd been naïve, but I'd never expected the kind of anger and visceral hate that people suddenly started spewing.

I had come to think of Middleburg as my home, and I didn't— and still don't—believe that most people in the town were racist. From the moment I'd moved there, I'd felt welcomed. Sure, there was the occasional ignorant comment, like the guy joking about chitlins at the hunt breakfast. But I believed that people would be able to see beyond our superficial differences to the bigger picture of what the inn could do for their town.

No matter how ugly the threats and comments became, I kept my head up. I tried to put myself in other people's shoes, to understand why they were responding so strongly. They were operating out of fear, uncomfortable with the changes that were coming to their hometown. I believed that if we could get past those old, ingrained feelings and face down that fear of change, we could create something great together. But as I tried to advance the dialogue, the fight intensified.

A woman at the PEC named Jeannie Perin started circulating petitions to stop me. Most of the signatures were from people who didn't even live in town, and some of them seemed to be made up altogether. In September, a group called Future of Middleburg held a meeting at Middleburg Elementary School, and about 250 people showed up. Everyone who got up to speak that night was opposed to the inn, and they talked at length about "preserving the character" of the town—which was code for exactly what you think it's code for. The group's website declared that the resort would "literally overwhelm and overshadow this special town we all share" and that it would "strangle Middleburg." In November, a group of town residents backed by the Future of Middleburg group filed an appeal to stop the project.

Once again, I heard that voice in my head. *What were you thinking, Sheila? Who do you think you are?* And worst of all: *You are going to fail.*

Bill and I were getting more serious about each other, and he could see the toll that this fight was taking on me. But beyond that, he saw that I was continuing to struggle with the emotional fallout of my years with Bob. When you're in a difficult marriage for more than three decades, everything doesn't magically become better the minute you divorce. As glad as I was to be away from Bob, and as happy as Bill made me, I was still a wreck.

I began having nightmares—terrifying dreams where something evil was chasing me or I was choking and couldn't get words out. Many nights, Bill had to shake me awake because I was weeping and crying out in my sleep. He was incredibly patient and loving with me, but in the dark of night, I never felt safe.

There were stretches when I plunged into depression or felt consumed by bitterness. Any time I thought about Bob and Debra together, I flared with anger all over again. I just couldn't get over what they had done and couldn't get past my feelings of humiliation and shame. And unfortunately, I sometimes took that out on Bill. Once, we were walking somewhere together and I got irritated at how slowly he was moving. "Come *on*, Bill!" I snapped. "I got stuff to do!"

He stopped dead and looked me in the eye. "Sheila," he said, "don't take out on me what you're feeling about Bob." He understood instinctively that my annoyance wasn't about him at all. Yet while he was willing to give me the benefit of the doubt, knowing what I'd been through, he wasn't willing to let me use him as a punching bag.

Other times, I pushed him about whether we were going to get married. "I mean, either we need to do this, or I need to move on," I told him. I had an intense sense of urgency, probably because I feared that he was going to leave me, and if he was, I needed it to happen sooner rather than later. I couldn't stand the thought of allowing myself to get close to this wonderful man, only to have him dump me and walk away. Down deep, I didn't believe he could love me, because I didn't feel I was worthy of love, no matter how many times he said it.

Whenever Bill would tell me he loved me, I didn't really believe him. Part of me thought he was gaslighting me as Bob had or playing me for a fool. *Poor, dumb Sheila really thinks she can get a man like Bill Newman?* The voices in my own head said things as cruel as anything Bob had ever said to me. I would ask Bill, "You say that, but do you really love me?" He'd say, "Yes, I really do." I would ask him why, because I still couldn't get my head around it. And eventually he would take my face in his hands and say, "Sheila. *You are worthy of being loved.*" It would take me years to believe him, but he never stopped saying it.

Bill was supportive, loving, and kind—but he was not stupid.

"There is no way we're getting married until you work some of this out," he told me. I didn't like it, but I knew he was probably right.

"Well, can we at least move in together?" I asked. I just needed to know that we were taking steps forward, because I was terrified that he would leave if we didn't.

"No, Sheila," he said. "I don't want Paige and Brett to just think I'm some guy swooping in here to shack up with their mom. Let's do this the right way." He told me I needed to come to a deeper understanding of what I'd been through and deal with the emotional fallout I was suffering. "You need to get help," he told me. "I think you should see a therapist, because nothing good can come for us until you get this previous relationship off your back."

Bill was absolutely right, of course. I did start seeing a therapist shortly after that, and as our sessions got going, I slowly began to understand what my years with Bob had done to me. Deep down, I had come to believe that I was a failure. That I was ugly. That I was worthless. I was consumed with bitterness and anger. And I always felt like people were laughing behind my back. *Stupid Sheila. What a fool.* I didn't know how to break that cycle—or if it could even be broken. Maybe I would just feel like this forever, an insecure mess of a woman.

Desperate to root out these feelings, I decided to try another kind of program. My friend Kim Tudor told me about Executive Success Programs, or ESP, a corporate retreat where high-level executives could get together in small groups to talk honestly about what was happening in their lives. Kim told me that Clare Bronfman, an heiress of the Seagram fortune who was also on the equestrian circuit, was involved in the organization, and she said the retreats were a safe place to vent and work out problems. I was anxious to keep my personal business private, especially since the *Washington Post* and other publications seemed so eager to publish gossip about Bob and me. This sounded like a good way to do that.

I joined a group of five people at the Carlyle Hotel in Manhattan for the first session. Most of the others were people I knew, or at least had met, so I felt comfortable pretty quickly. We did a weekend workshop, opening up about our problems, pains, grief, and whatever else was on our minds, occasionally breaking into one-on-one sessions. It was hard for me to talk about what I'd gone through, as I still felt so burdened by shame and humiliation. But I tried to open up as much as I could, and by the end of the weekend it felt like I'd actually made some progress.

About a month later, I signed up for a second session. This one started out similar to the first one, but after a day of prying myself open, talking about my feelings, and discussing details of my life that I had never shared before, my head started pounding. It got worse and worse, slamming into a full-on migraine, and the pain got so severe that I started throwing up. I told Kim I was afraid I was having a brain hemorrhage, and she checked in with the ESP staff. They said I was just "releasing toxicity" and that this purge was a good thing. I don't know about all that, but it was the sickest I have ever been. I vomited all night, but the next day I did actually feel significantly better.

That was the end of my experimenting with ESP, though. I didn't do any more sessions after that weekend and never had anything else to do with the organization. Many years later, it would end up morphing into a cult called NXIVM, and when news broke about the crazy behavior of its leaders—brainwashing young women, enslaving them, and even branding their bodies—some newspapers reported

SHEILA JOHNSON

that I had been involved with the cult. I wasn't, but the association is out there on the Internet and will be forever, I suppose. Those two sessions were the extent of my involvement, during a time when I was struggling to find some way—any way—out of the emotional turmoil I was in.

After the divorce, I moved my mother from Illinois to Virginia to live with the kids and me. She was in her seventies now and not in the best of health, but I didn't bring her to Salamander Farm to take care of her. I brought her because I needed her.

She didn't live in the house with us but had her own little place a ways off, nestled among the trees on my property. There was a front porch where she could sit and watch the sunset or see the deer out prancing in the woods. She'd come take her meals at the house, and I loved having her right there with me. I hadn't spent so much time with her since I'd left Maywood at age seventeen, and now that my divorce was final, I at last felt free to talk with her about everything that had gone on.

If anyone could understand what I had been through, it was my mother. She prayed with me, she hugged me, she felt my pain. Four decades earlier, I had cradled my mother on her kitchen floor while she wept and wailed. Now she did the same for me. We had come full circle.

I remember two moments in particular from that time. Once, she said to me, "Bob needs to find God."

I just rolled my eyes. "Mom," I said, "he can literally quote the Bible."

"You know what, Sheila?" she replied, deadpan. "The devil can quote the Bible." That's what my mom thought of Bob.

The other moment happened on a day when I was feeling particularly down. My mother saw me moping around the house, and she came and took me by the shoulders. "Listen to me, Sheila," she said. "You are not going to let this defeat you. You have too much to give to this world."

I just looked at her, my eyes welling up with tears. I didn't even have the strength to answer.

"You are going to get your power back," she said. "Believe it."

I could only hope that she was right.

On a crisp winter day in February 2004, I felt like I got a little glimpse of that power. After months of renovations, upgrades, painting, and menu planning, Market Salamander was finally ready to open.

When I bought the Powder Horn Gun & Antique shop, I had no idea what kind of condition the building was in. I hired a team of contractors to assess it, and one of them called me to say, "You need to come see this." To all our surprise, it turned out that the building was actually a shell that had been constructed over a historic old home.

We tore down those outer walls, revealing the beautiful bones of the house, and then I hired designers and artists to turn it into a French-style market. I wanted the interior to feel like a Parisian street scene, complete with cobblestones and a quaint storefront where people could browse the charcuterie, cheeses, and fresh-baked pastries. Bistro tables and chairs rounded out the scene, and I made sure we had excellent Wi-Fi and rich espresso drinks, along with a big selection of local wines. Basically, I made Market Salamander into exactly the kind of bistro you'd visit on a trip to France.

People in town responded rapturously to the market's opening, which was a huge relief. I had felt really stung by the backlash to my plans for the inn, so it was encouraging to see people buying our fried oysters and enjoying the warm and welcoming world we'd created there. I watched it all with one of my new hires, a young woman named Giardy Ritz. She'd been with us only for a couple of months, but I already felt like I could trust her with just about anything—and sure enough, she would go on to become one of my best hires, my chief of staff, and a close confidante.

Standing there with Giardy, watching crowds of people enjoying the market, I dared to hope that maybe our success here would turn the tide of opinion on the inn too. But as I soon found out, it wouldn't be that easy. Not even close.

Twelve

"THAT WOMAN"

"You're going to need more rooms."

I took a deep breath, then looked at the man who'd just uttered these words. His name was Prem Devadas, he was the managing director at Kiawah Island Resort in South Carolina, and he was confirming something I'd already begun to suspect. My planned fifty-eight-room inn would almost certainly lose money given how expensive it is to run a luxury property.

"How many more?" I asked Prem. I was busy fighting local backlash over a fifty-eight-room inn, which had already grown from my original plan for forty rooms. How much bigger did this thing need to be?

"I'd say a hundred twenty rooms is the minimum in order to support the level of luxury you're planning," he said. I had told Prem my plans for the resort, from hiring the top architectural firm WATG and a superstar designer named Thomas Pheasant, to constructing a spa, a ballroom, and an equestrian center. I wanted Salamander to be absolutely top-of-the-line in every possible way, including the furnishings, décor, and landscaping, but that costs money. With the inn having just fifty-eight rooms in a French-château-style setting, it would be almost impossible for it to generate enough profit to sustain the level of quality I wanted. And quality was one thing I wasn't willing to compromise on.

Prem had a lot more experience than I did in the hotel business, which is why I had come to him for advice. He had just taken the Kiawah Island Resort through the same kind of approvals fight that I was facing, and he was familiar with Middleburg, having grown up in Washington, DC. I decided that advice was nice, but what I really wanted was to hire him to lead my new company, Salamander LLC. Sandy Ain had vouched for Prem, and he seemed like a smart, hard worker and a good fit.

And if I had to increase the number of rooms again, I was going to need him.

Not long after Prem came to work with me, my office got a call from Robert Duvall. He wanted to drop by with his wife, the Argentine actress Luciana Pedraza, to talk about the plans for what we were now calling Salamander Resort & Spa.

Duvall was in his seventies, and he'd lived on the 360-acre Byrnley Farm in nearby The Plains for over a decade. It was a gorgeous piece of land, with an old farmhouse that he'd turned into a dance studio. He and his wife were tango aficionados, and they loved to give friends lessons and hold dance parties at their property. Duvall also loved horses, and he had watched Paige in equestrian competitions before, so we had met a few times.

But today, he didn't want to talk about horses or tango or our farms. He and Luciana were concerned about my plans for the resort, and they wanted to discuss it. I knew I'd have an uphill climb to win them over, since Luciana had already publicly opposed the project, so I asked Prem to come and help me make my case.

I walked everyone into the house, past those big picture windows with views of the Shenandoah, and the four of us sat down to talk. Prem and I described the basics, including the proposed layout and design as well as nuts-and-bolts details about water, electricity, sewage, and traffic management. But I also wanted them to understand my deeper motivation behind the project. My vision was for Salamander Resort & Spa to be a place where *everyone* could come and feel comfortable—a place that reflected the local equestrian culture but also had a diverse array of art, musical performances, and culinary offerings. I wanted Salamander to feel like a home away from home, a sanctuary where people could come have a glass of wine, sit by a firepit with friends, or hike the trails and enjoy the natural beauty.

I truly believed that if we did this right, the resort would become Middleburg's living room. And if we did it *really* right, in a few years, people wouldn't even have any recollection of what all the fuss was about. That was the vision Prem and I laid out, and when we were done, Duvall actually smiled a little.

"Well, that doesn't sound too bad," he said. His wife threw him a look, then coolly turned her attention to Prem and me. She then proceeded to rip the project three ways from Sunday, saying that it would destroy Middleburg, ruin the natural beauty of the area, damage local businesses, cause horrible traffic jams—pretty much every terrible outcome you can imagine. Duvall had bought a diner called the Rail Stop in The Plains a few years earlier, and they used that as an example of how I should "keep things simple," which apparently meant building and changing as little as possible.

Prem kept his cool, but I could see that he'd underestimated the amount of pushback we would be getting. After his wife spoke, Duvall looked at me and said, "Of course, if you do manage to build this resort, we'll never set foot in it."

"I'm sorry to hear that," I said. And I was. Not only because having Robert Duvall's backing would have helped us in our efforts to win local support, but because I knew the resort was going to be the kind of place he would love.

We all shook hands at the end of the meeting, and after they had left, Prem said, "Wow. I understand what we're facing now." A series of Middleburg town council votes was coming up that would determine whether we had the local government's backing, and if our arguments fell on similarly deaf ears leading up to those meetings, we might be in trouble.

It was time to figure out another strategy.

All 340 acres of the Harriman property were in Loudoun County, but only 88 of them were situated within the town boundaries of Middleburg. We could have built the resort on the non-Middleburg part of the land, which would have required permission only from the Loudoun County board of supervisors, a pro-development group that had already expressed its support. But that would have placed the resort way out in the woods, too far for guests to walk into town. We really needed to position it on those Middleburg acres—but that would unfortunately open a whole new can of worms.

The Middleburg town council didn't like the idea of the resort.

A few council members were open to discussing it with us, but the majority seemed to have made up their minds in opposition. Having been lobbied by the Piedmont Environmental Council and other groups, and seeing all those signs and petitions and bumper stickers popping up, they were nervous. What if the naysayers were right? What if the council members approved a 120-room resort right on the edge of town and it ruined Middleburg? It would be easier and safer just to say no.

Not long after Prem agreed to join my company, he'd made some calls to his contacts in Virginia to research the resort project. What he heard was discouraging. "We have it on very good authority," one person told him, "that this project will never be approved." He informed me about that conversation, but that only made me more determined. "I have confidence in you. And I have confidence in me," I told Prem. "We are *going to get this done.*"

We needed to find a way to sweeten the pot for Middleburg. The council knew that the resort would bring in tourist revenue and tax dollars, but that apparently wasn't enough. Was there anything else we could offer? As it turned out, there was.

The town relied on a twenty-year-old wastewater treatment plant that was falling to pieces. This thing was truly on its last legs, and there was no money in the budget to do anything about it. The total population of Middleburg was only 632 people, and out of those, only 435 were paying customers of the wastewater plant. Their bills already averaged nearly three times the amount paid by their neighbors in nearby towns such as Leesburg, and the quality of service was still terrible. But Middleburg kept on limping along with it because a new sewer plant would cost more than $4 million. Where on earth would that kind of money come from, for a plant that served just 435 people?

Well, our resort would obviously need a highly functioning wastewater plant. So I decided to offer a brand-new, state-of-the-art one to the town, in exchange for boundary line changes that would allow us to build in the spot we wanted. Those changes would expand Middleburg's footprint to include the entire 340 acres of our property, which would also bring in more tax revenue for the town. This wasn't a sexy solution, but horse trades in local politics rarely are. The main thing was, it would give all of us what we needed.

Prem and I got to work, calling the town council members and explaining our plan. We worked with them to craft a memorandum of understanding (MOU) laying out all the terms. And in an effort to be transparent, we launched a public-outreach campaign, giving presentations at public meetings, contacting residents, and inviting comments from anyone who wanted to weigh in on the plan. The council members spent hours behind the scenes discussing our offer, engaging in a hot debate over whether this would be a boon for the town or destroy it. Everyone seemed to have an opinion, and as the months went by, the council was still leaning toward voting no.

After about six months of lobbying, cajoling, and maneuvering on all sides, the town council finally scheduled a vote. Mayor Dimos added it to the agenda for the next regular meeting, which was to be held on July 14, 2005.

In the days leading up to that meeting, I was an absolute wreck. I was beyond nervous, afraid that this town I loved would shoot down my dream. For three years, I had been working night and day to create a beautiful, welcoming, one-of-a-kind resort. But it had come to represent much more than that to me.

Salamander Resort & Spa was my first truly big undertaking since divorcing Bob. I wanted to build it for its own sake, but I also had something to prove. After all those years of toiling to build BET, I still never seemed to get credit for anything other than being Bob Johnson's wife. Even the cover of Brett Pulley's book, *The Billion Dollar BET*, turned out to be a close-up photo of Bob sitting on a conference table and looking smug, like he owned the world and you were just his guest there. Nobody thought I could be a success in business, because nobody knew what I'd done at BET, or that I had built my own lucrative music business in the 1970s and '80s.

I could still hear Bob's voice in my head, telling me I was going to fail. And if that wasn't enough, I often heard it from Bob himself, whom I unfortunately still had to see because we were co-parenting our kids. He seemed to enjoy the battle over the resort, and whenever he'd come to the farm to pick up Paige or Brett, he'd be sure to tell me how much I was doing wrong. He was constantly in my business, just showing up at the house and dropping his opinions everywhere. I finally told him he wasn't allowed on the property without my permission and said that I would gladly have my security team escort him off. But even over the phone, he'd find a way to undercut me and make me doubt myself.

Because of all this, the upcoming town council vote felt like more than a referendum on the resort; it felt like a judgment on who I was as a person and a businesswoman. I had made some bad decisions in my life, and as a result I had come to doubt my own instincts. The big decisions I'd made over these last three years—moving full-time to Middleburg, investing heavily in the community, and choosing to fight for this resort—had felt right to me at the time. Yet given everything that had happened over the past three decades, how could I not doubt myself?

If the council voted us down, how would I ever show my face in

Middleburg again? If they pushed away the more than $4 million I was offering them, how could it mean anything other than abject rejection? I'd been trying so hard to crawl out of that dark emotional hole, and this vote could knock me right back into it. If I lost, I would feel like I had lost my home. And the thought of that scared me half to death.

A few days before the meeting, I asked Prem whether I should be there. I wanted to go, but would my presence help or hurt? All I cared about was winning the vote—not making a statement, or showing my face, or achieving some kind of moral victory. If Prem thought my being there would help us win, I would go. If not, I wouldn't.

"I have to be honest with you, Sheila," he said. "I don't think we're going to win either way. From what I can tell, we don't have the votes." There were seven members on the Middleburg town council, and at least four were expected to vote against us. "But I still think you should come," he continued. "There's going to be a big show of opposition, and it's important to face people in person."

He then explained that even if we lost this vote, it didn't mean the resort was dead. We could rejigger our plans, submit another MOU, and ask for another vote down the road. I absolutely dreaded that thought but realized that Prem was right. This was my project, and I couldn't just hide out at my farm while the town made its decision. I needed to find the courage to look my fellow townspeople in the eye, regardless of how the vote ultimately went.

The meeting fell on a Thursday evening, and the small room in the Middleburg town hall was crammed with people. It seemed like half the town had come out, along with reporters and photographers covering the story. A long, curved table was at the front, and the seven council members were sitting there with Mayor Dimos, who would conduct the meeting. Looming behind them was the official Middleburg seal, with an image of a fox and the town's motto: *Semel et Semper*, Latin for "Once and Always." Prem and I found seats over on the side, and I sat fiddling with my hands, wishing the damn meeting would start already.

The mood in the room was anxious as Mayor Dimos called the meeting to order. Ours was the second item on the agenda, so we had to wait while the council took care of some other piece of business first. Finally, the mayor opened discussion on Salamander Resort and our proposed memorandum of understanding. He invited public comment—and oh my god, the floodgates opened. For the next two hours, people got up and absolutely let their opinions fly. And some of them were colorful, to say the least.

The first few speakers were in favor of the resort. One of them held up two brown bags, one from Market Salamander and another just a plain bag. He said the council's decision was like choosing a lunch special, either the Salamander version or the "developer's delight," which came with housing sprawl and negative environmental impact. He went on and on from there, explaining all the reasons why the council members should vote yes "loud and clear!" He blew past the three-minute time limit, going on for so long that Mayor Dimos then declared he would allow others to speak longer than the allotted three minutes as well.

The next few speakers were mostly in favor, too, for all kinds of reasons. People liked the idea of the new wastewater treatment plant, they welcomed the tax revenues, and they wanted the town to have some control. "A vote in favor means the town gets to keep its thumb in the pie!" one woman declared. This was going well so far—but I knew it couldn't last. And it didn't.

Now the naysayers took their turns. A couple of them complained about the size of the resort, the plan for a spa, the impact on trees, and even the uncertainty of what might happen if I later sold the property. People said they were nervous and that the town was giving up too much control. I wanted to stand up and answer all their questions, but I held my peace. As Prem and I had discussed, it was important to remain unemotional and let the discussion take its course. The townspeople wanted to be heard, and they deserved to be heard. So I sat there, quiet as a lamb but screaming inside.

Then Sam Huff stood up.

Sam was a local hero, a star football player for the Washington Redskins in the 1960s who now worked as a color commentator on their games. He had lived in Middleburg for decades, breeding Thoroughbred racehorses on his farm and popping down regularly to the Red Fox Inn for breakfast. He was easy to spot, a big man with a big smile. People in town loved Sam, but as we were all about to find out, Sam did *not* love me or my project.

"Middleburg is the greatest little town in America," Sam boomed. "But Paul Mellon would be turning over in his grave over this resort. Because the town is selling out." Paul Mellon, of course, was the heir to the Mellon banking fortune, and he had been a breeder of Thoroughbred horses in nearby Upperville, Virginia. He had also been dead for six years, so I wasn't sure why he should be the arbiter of anything. But Sam was just getting started.

"Paul Mellon never tried to buy this town," he said. "Jack Kent Cooke never tried to buy this town." He rambled on that he had recently been to an event at the Lansdowne Resort in Leesburg and

WALK THROUGH FIRE

had seen several members of the NFL Hall of Fame there. "Sheila Johnson will *never* get Hall of Fame members at her resort," he declared. "In fact, I don't know what the hell she wants, and I'm not sure she knows what she wants. But Middleburg does not sell out to anyone."

By this point, my blood was boiling. I was trying to keep my expression neutral, but what I really wanted was to jump up and get in the face of this arrogant man who seemed to believe that only *he* knew what was best for Middleburg. You could say there was a subtext to his words, but there was really no *sub* about it. Because it was plain as day what Sam Huff was saying—that Middleburg belonged to people who looked like him, not like me. And if there was any doubt, he dispelled it with his final words.

"Do not sell Middleburg out to *that woman*," he said, pointing at me, "or to anybody else . . . Mr. Mellon would be proud of everyone if we don't."

Now I was furious, but Sam's insults and criticism were only the beginning, as more naysayers followed him. One woman said I was setting an "extremely dangerous precedent." Another claimed I was "using threats and blackmail" to get my way. An elderly man stood up and said that poor development would "do more harm to Middleburg than the Union did during the Civil War."

One after another, the town's citizens got up to offer their unvarnished opinions. Some were in favor, others were opposed, and a few still hadn't made up their minds but wanted to say their piece anyway. For two hours I sat in my folding chair, listening to everybody under the sun say what they thought about my project. Then we finally got to the last speaker, a woman who declared that adding 250 acres to the town was scary, that Salamander was issuing ultimatums, and that I had been threatening people if we didn't get our way. Hers was the last public comment, and at nine thirty p.m., Mayor Dimos declared a ten-minute recess, probably to break the tension in the room.

When the meeting reconvened at a quarter to ten, it was finally time for the town staff and council members to give their statements. But first, the mayor invited our side to speak. Prem and our attorney, Jonathan Rak, reiterated everything the town had to gain, including a half million dollars in annual tax revenue, the multimillion-dollar wastewater treatment plant, and town control over all 340 acres of the property. When they sat down, I felt like we had done everything we could possibly do. And then it was time for the vote.

The first council member to speak, Vice Mayor Betsy Davis, declared that "change is good when it is controlled," then said she resented any suggestion that the council would be selling out the town. She said her vote was a yes.

The next two members, Helen Hyre and Bundles Murdock, both said they were more concerned with preserving the town than inviting development, so they were voting no. The fourth, Darlene Kirk, read from a written statement saying that we had answered her concerns and that she would vote yes. We were tied, 2–2.

The next vote, from Margaret New, was a no, in part, she said, because "the land in question is hallowed ground." Now we were down 2–3, and there were only two votes left. We would need them both to win.

Mark Snyder was the next council member, and he was a wild card. Nobody knew how he was going to vote, and he'd seemed to go back and forth several times in the weeks leading up to the meeting. I held my breath as he began speaking, especially when he declared he "needed some help from Mr. Rak and Mr. Devadas." *What kind of help?* Mark wanted us to change a couple of minor points in the MOU, and he asked for one item about water fees to be struck. If we agreed to those changes, he said, he would vote yes. And that would make it 3–3.

The final vote came from a woman named Eura Lewis. Everyone in the room scooched to the edges of their chairs as she pulled out her prepared statement. Eura opened by talking about a seminar held back in 1998 for some reason, and I wished she would get to the point. "I have been following very closely all the MOUs, five of them to be exact," she said, adding, "Each one offers and states the same agreements, with the exception of 3(d), and what it states now we have taken out and put back in again."

What? I was losing the thread, but thankfully, she finally found her way to the issue at hand. And she did it in a strangely colorful way.

"The memorandum of understanding is an excellent one to use or work with," she said. "The Salamander attorney and team, along with our excellent, exuberant, luscious attorney Ms. Whiting, have done a magnificent job in keeping this agreement to meet the parties' desire." *Luscious?* Prem and I looked at each other, then back at Eura. "I believe this agreement has laid the ground foundation for the 'bay,' knowing full well that the 'ocean' lies ahead," she said, then concluded, "My vote is YES."

I burst into tears. Four votes to three—we had done it! Prem and Jonathan and I hugged each other, and the people who had been opposed started hurrying for the exit. Others came up to shake my hand and offer congratulations, which I accepted through sobs. I felt like the weight of the world had finally, mercifully, been lifted from my shoulders.

I wasn't an idiot. I wasn't a failure. My adopted hometown had my back. There would be a few more town council votes over the next two years, clarifying details of the project, but 2005 was the turning point. It's the year when I knew my dream of Salamander Resort would become a reality.

It's also the year when another dream came true.

On September 24, 2005, in front of seven hundred guests at my beloved Salamander Farm, Bill and I became husband and wife. I figured that since my first wedding had been so small and ended so badly, I might as well do this one up right. I felt so lucky to have found Bill again after all those years, and we definitely had a whole lot to celebrate.

From the beginning, Bill had said he needed me to get to a better place emotionally before we could marry. I knew he was right, so I had worked hard to sort through the trauma of my first marriage. Seeing a therapist had helped a tremendous amount, and of course the longer Bill and I were together, the more secure I felt in our relationship. I didn't know when he would feel like I'd made enough progress, but I felt good about the direction in which we were heading.

One night in December 2004, we were relaxing at Bill's house after having dinner out. We started talking about how far I had come in the two-plus years since my divorce. "You know, I've been working hard to get my life together," I told him.

"So you have," he said, nodding.

"I know you don't want to get married until I'm better," I said. "Maybe one day soon you'll feel like I'm there." Before, I might have pushed him to propose. But now I felt calmer, like it would happen whenever it was meant to happen.

"Excuse me a minute," Bill said, and he got up from the table. I asked him where he was going, and he just said, "I'll be right back." He went upstairs, and when he came back, he started sinking toward the floor. *Oh my god—is he fainting?* I was about to jump out of my chair when I saw that he had gone down on one knee, which, let's be honest, was not the easiest thing for a big man who'd had knee surgery.

"Sheila," he said, smiling sweetly, "will you marry me?" And he held out a box with an emerald-cut diamond ring. I started crying and immediately said yes. He told me later that he hadn't meant to ask me that night, intending to plan a more romantic evening around the proposal. But he's a man who operates on instinct, and the time just seemed right.

I was ecstatic, yet also nervous about breaking the news to Brett and Paige. They both really liked Bill, but it's difficult to see your divorced parents moving on. I suspect every child of divorce harbors a deep-down wish that their parents might one day get back together, no matter how bad the marriage actually was. Sure enough, when I told Paige we were engaged, she started crying. "I'm happy for you," she said, "but I'm also sad."

My mother, on the other hand, was straight-up thrilled when I told her. And then she got a little twinkle in her eye.

"Sheila," she said, "have you tasted the milk?"

"Have I *what*, now?" I said. Surely she wasn't saying what I thought she was saying.

But she was. "You know what I mean," she said, laughing. "Girl, you got to make sure it's good!"

I have no idea where she got that expression from, and I was mildly horrified to be having this discussion with my mother, but in the end

I couldn't help but laugh with her. She and I both had walked through fire, and we'd been through more highs and lows together than I could count. But we'd made it to the other side, and we had always been there for each other. I was so happy that she was living with me as she entered the autumn of her life, and that we had seen each other get to a better place.

Bill and I started out with a guest list of one hundred people, but the more I thought about it, the more I wanted to share this day with everyone who had been important to us over the years. Bill had friends in the law community, Virginia politics, and the theater, and I had friends from my life in music, philanthropy, and business. We weren't a couple of kids getting married—we were people in our fifties who had lived full and busy lives. And so we expanded our guest list into what Bill jokingly called "a cast of thousands."

I had wanted to do all the planning and put on the wedding myself, but Bill just shook his head. He had been asked to officiate weddings before, and he had seen how much work it took to throw that big of a party for hundreds of people. "You've got to hire somebody," he said. So I brought in a wedding planner named Preston Bailey, which turned out to be the best decision I could have made. Preston made our wedding day into a dream, turning the riding arena at Salamander Farm into a little white chapel, planning a steak-and-lobster dinner for seven hundred, shipping in thousands of flowers, and building a translucent dance floor for the reception. We also had a four-hundred-pound tiered wedding cake designed by Sylvia Weinstock.

Brett walked me down the aisle, and Paige was my maid of honor. I felt like I might burst from happiness when I saw Bill standing at the altar, looking so handsome in his black-tie tuxedo. I was wearing a Bob Mackie gown that I loved, even though my mother said, "Honey, that dress is cut too low." I just smiled and said, "Listen, Mom, it's just a little cleavage. I've got to stay young, you know."

The wedding was extravagant, but after everything I'd been through to get to this moment, I wanted to celebrate. But the most memorable part for me was not the fancy hors d'oeuvres or the table settings or the lantern-lined walk. It was the moment when Bill and I stood at the altar and spoke our very simple vows.

We looked at each other, holding hands, and Bill spoke first. "I love Sheila, and I want to marry her," he said. I let the words wash over me, then said, "I love Bill, and I want to marry him." Our officiant, the Reverend William MacDonald Murray, pronounced us husband and wife, and we kissed to make it official. I hadn't felt so happy in a long, long time. But more than that, I finally felt safe.

Thirteen

ZERO TO SIXTY

One afternoon in the spring of 2005, I went to downtown DC for a luncheon hosted by Irene Pollin. Irene was a big philanthropist in town, and she and her husband, Abe, owned a farm not far from mine in Virginia. "Abe wants to talk with you about something," she said. "Would you be able to go by his office next Tuesday at two p.m.?"

What could this be about? Abe Pollin was a beloved local figure, the owner of the Washington Wizards NBA team, the Washington Capitals NHL team, and the Washington Mystics WNBA team. He was also the man who had revitalized DC's Chinatown neighborhood by building a brand-new arena there on his own dime. Abe was in his eighties now, and he and Irene had been married for sixty years. I adored them both and loved having them as my neighbors in horse country. But I couldn't figure what Abe wanted to talk about that was so important.

The next Tuesday, I showed up at his office, and as I walked in,

Abe smiled so big. "Sheila," he said, "I want you to be the face of the Mystics."

"You mean, you want me to do an ad for them?" I asked. This was an unexpected request, but I was game. I had always been a big fan of women's sports and a supporter of Title IX, so I was happy to help promote the team.

"No, no," Abe said, and laughed. "I want you to *own* them."

I'm sorry, what? No small talk, no preamble—just a straight-up offer to sell me the team. "Why me?" I asked.

"Why not you?" Abe responded—which was an answer I loved, as he undoubtedly knew I would.

I was intrigued, but I also knew that Abe was a smart business-man, so there had to be a reason he was trying to unload the team. "Does it make any money?" I asked him.

"I'll give you all the financials," he said. "This is highly confiden-tial, so don't speak of it to anyone. Have a look, and let me know if you're interested."

Of course, the minute I was out of Abe's office, I called Sandy Ain. "Guess what," I said. "Abe Pollin has just offered me the Mystics."

Sandy didn't hesitate. "Don't do it, Sheila," he said. "The Mystics don't make any money. None of the WNBA teams do."

This was disappointing to hear. I'd gotten excited at the idea of owning a professional women's sports team—but as a business-woman, I knew it made no sense for me to throw my cash into a known money pit. If there was one thing I had learned, though, it was that business isn't only about numbers and spreadsheets. It's about people, and it's about creativity. Was there some way I could make this work for me financially? I decided I had to try.

"Doesn't Ted Leonsis have right of first refusal for the Wizards when Abe Pollin passes?" I asked. Sandy confirmed that he did. "I'm coming over," I told him. "I think I know how to do this, but I need to talk with Ted." I went straight to Sandy's office, and we got him on speakerphone right away.

Ted had made his money in the Internet boom, selling his startup company to AOL, then joining them as an executive as their stock rose. He and the Pollins were partners in Lincoln Holdings, the company that owned the three sports teams. If I could get Ted on board with this new plan I had, there was a way to make this purchase work.

"Ted," I said, "between you and me, Abe has just offered me the Washington Mystics." Through the speakerphone, I could hear Ted groan, which made me laugh. "I know, I know," I said. "Sandy Ain and I have looked at the numbers. It makes no sense. But . . . I have a different idea." And then I laid out my plan.

"I have the financial capacity to buy into the Wizards and Capitals too," I told him. "And if I did that, you'd have a woman and an African American as an owner, which is good for everybody." There were precious few Black owners in American professional sports, almost no women, and no Black women at all. It was past time to rectify that—and Ted knew it. "I don't want to pay a penny less or a penny more than any other owners," I said. "And you can get a twofer. No other franchise has that."

"You know," Ted said, "that's not a bad idea. Let me bring it to the other owners and I'll get back to you." They loved the idea, and so did the leagues' executives. And that's how I became the only Black female co-owner of three professional sports teams. I was excited to be involved with the Wizards and Caps, but I was *thrilled* to own the Mystics, a team of fantastic women who would end up stealing my heart.

There's another part to this story. It starts back in the early nineties, when Bob and I were still married and had made some money from the BET IPO.

Bob and I had known the Pollins for years, and every time we saw them, Bob would tell Abe he wanted to own the Wizards, which were then called the Bullets. This was his long-held dream, not only personally but as the cofounder of BET. "Washington is a Black city," he told Abe. "And the NBA is a Black league. So it makes sense that the Bullets should have a Black owner." His goal was to brand the Bullets as "Black America's team," broadcast their games on BET, and sell merchandise all over the country.

Bob's idea was a good one, but he couldn't make any headway with Abe. So in 1994, he decided to play hardball. Abe was planning to build a new arena, and he was counting on a big pot of municipal funding that the DC government had promised him. Bob used that as a way to undercut him. He told city officials that Abe should pay for the arena himself, hired lobbyists to fight against Abe's deal, and even sued to stop it from going forward. DC was strapped for cash in those days, so Bob's old friend Mayor Marion Barry eventually agreed, withdrawing the offer of public funds. Thanks in large part to Bob, Abe had no choice but to pay for the new $200 million arena himself. And Abe would never forget it.

The night before our press conference announcing the deal, I decided I should give Bob a heads-up. I called him and said, "I just want you to know that I've bought into Lincoln Holdings. I'm going to be an owner of the Wizards, Caps, and Mystics."

"*What!?*" he snapped. "Sheila, what are you talking about?" I repeated what I'd told him, and he said, "Don't do this to me, Sheila. *Do not do this to me.*"

"Bob, it's already done," I said. "We're announcing it tomorrow."

Oh my god, you would have thought I had burned his house down, he was so angry. He went on and on until I said, "I've got to go." Then he called me a couple more times before I finally just stopped picking up the phone.

Here's what's funny, though. When I pursued this deal with Abe and Ted, I wasn't even thinking about the fact that Bob wanted the team so badly in the nineties. In fact, I initially didn't make the connection that this was why Bob was so angry. But others certainly had made it. A few weeks later, when Kojo Nnamdi of WAMU interviewed me for his show, he laughed and said Abe was "sticking a pin into his old nemesis Bob Johnson." Kojo even seemed to think that Abe might have done this deal with me specifically to get back at Bob.

I don't know about all that, because Abe Pollin was a good man and not a vindictive type of person. He was also a savvy businessman, and he knew this was a smart deal. If Bob ended up getting his feelings hurt, that wasn't Abe's problem.

And you know what? It wasn't mine either.

The year 2005 marked a turning point for me in so many ways. Winning that 4–3 vote for the resort, buying into the sports teams, and marrying Bill were big, wonderful, life-changing events that all happened within months of each other. Three years after finalizing my divorce from Bob, I felt like I was beginning to come into my own as a woman and a businessperson. And then, right at the end of the year, one more meaningful event happened—a connection that would truly give me a new perspective on life.

A man named Dale Mott called my office, asking if we could meet to talk about a nonprofit called CARE. I got these kinds of calls all the time, mostly from people looking for cash donations. But Dale, who was the organization's development director, said he wasn't just interested in money. He wanted me to become involved in a more direct and personal way. I was intrigued, so I invited him to come to Middleburg and tell me more.

Dale drove out from DC early one morning, meeting me at Market Salamander. He must have been nervous, because as we sat down at a café table, I could see he'd forgotten to remove the tag on his suit jacket. I gently pointed it out, and the poor guy turned the color of a beet. He was really embarrassed, but we ended up laughing about it, and from that moment I decided I liked Dale Mott.

What I really liked, though, was what Dale was proposing. CARE, which stands for Cooperative for Assistance and Relief Everywhere, is an international humanitarian organization that provides emergency aid and assistance to people around the world. They run programs fighting poverty, providing safe water and food, and encouraging economic development, among many other initiatives. But the programs Dale wanted to talk about focused on women's empowerment.

CARE had multiple programs aimed at helping girls and women. They provided microfinancing for women in developing countries to start their own businesses. They worked to stop human trafficking, gender discrimination, and violence against women. Dale told me that women and girls make up more than 60 percent of people who suffer from hunger and 70 percent of people in extreme poverty. And more than a third of women worldwide have suffered physical or sexual violence—or both.

"Okay, I'm in," I said after about ten minutes of hearing Dale talk.

"Don't you want to see the PowerPoint I made?" he asked.

"Nope," I said. "Just tell me how I can help."

As Dale had been speaking, I'd been thinking about my own life and how it compared with what he was describing. Yes, I had been miserable in the years around my divorce. My sense of self was deeply shaken, and I cried more tears than I ever thought possible. But I had never wondered where my next meal was coming from. I had never been beaten or trafficked. I had never faced the kind of crushing oppression, poverty, and hopelessness that so many women face every single day.

Dale said that CARE wanted me to become a global ambassador. He asked if I'd be willing to travel to other countries to work on projects, and to become a face of their women's empowerment program. I told him I'd be thrilled. For years, I had been focusing inward on my own troubles. That may have been necessary in order to heal—but now I was ready to start looking outward, to help other women. Working with CARE would be the perfect opportunity to do that.

I had a private plane at that point, and I told Dale we could use it in support of the programs. We started traveling all over the globe, to places like Guatemala, Ecuador, Rwanda, Tanzania, South Africa—all countries where CARE was actively supporting women in need. Bill came on many of these trips, and we were often joined by Dale Mott as well as the organization's incoming president and CEO, Dr. Helene Gayle. Dr. Gayle was a force of nature, an energetic and innovative leader who wanted to take CARE to the next level. I felt incredibly lucky to be a part of a strategy that would change so many lives—including my own.

In Guatemala, we met with a group of women who were part of CARE's microfinance program. CARE would provide very small loans for them to start their own businesses—selling flowers, for example, or sewing clothes—so they could support themselves rather than having to depend on men to survive. As part of an empowerment course, we gave the women mirrors, then asked what they saw. My heart ached as I heard so many of these women saying they didn't like what they saw in the mirror. And I could relate strongly to what they were feeling, having been there myself just a few years earlier. "I believe in you," I would tell these women. "You are powerful." I was channeling my mother's own words to me, and it felt good to be paying that message forward.

In Rwanda, we went to remote villages where women were living on less than a dollar a day. "Can't I just give them money?" I asked Dale. "No, Sheila," he said. "That's not our mission." He explained that CARE's programs weren't about handing women money that would last for a finite time; they were about jump-starting women's ability to support themselves in the long term. In one village, we provided goats to a group of women, so they could sell the milk and, later, the meat. In another, I sat with women on the red dirt outside their huts as they met to collect microloan payments. It was these microfinancing collectives that truly opened my eyes to what women can do for each other.

Women living in poverty can't get traditional loans, not only because of sexist banking practices but also because they have nothing to offer as collateral. In microfinance programs, groups of women commit to supporting each other and being responsible for each other's loans. They meet every few days to talk about how their small businesses are doing, make loan payments, and offer encouragement if anyone needs help. The women succeed only if they support each other—and in that, I saw a lesson for all of us, no matter our socio-economic position. Women have got to bond together, to help each other break the dependency so many of us have on men.

Meeting these women, and seeing how they lifted each other out of dependency, was like seeing my own life in a microcosm. When I saw them encouraging each other, touching hands, sharing their worries, I thought of the village of women who had helped me: Susan Starrett, Mary Henderson, my mother. On the surface, my life was profoundly different from the lives of these Rwandan women. But deeper down, we were members of the same sisterhood. We had gone through many of the same things. We understood each other. And that made me ever more determined to help them in any way I could.

Dale saw the effect that all this was having on me, so he took a minute to explain why CARE was specifically focused on women. They took responsibility for their families and communities in ways the men often did not. They supported each other with empathy and strength. And they took care of the next generation—the children who might actually have a chance to grow out of poverty. Dale told me about a saying he'd heard. "Give a man a dollar, and he'll spend it on himself," he told me. "Give a woman a dollar, and she'll spend it on the community."

Well, I decided we needed to get a lot more dollars together to help out these women. When CARE announced a new campaign called "I Am Powerful," Dr. Gayle asked if I would become a public face of the effort. I agreed and offered a $4 million matching grant to help raise funds. Within two months, that matching grant had generated $6 million in donations, making a total of $10 million for the program. The tagline was "She has the power to change your world. You have the power to help her do it." I felt that down to my roots.

At this point in my life, I hadn't talked to many people about what I'd gone through with my ex-husband. But one night in New York, as I prepared to present an award to Dr. Gayle, I found myself overwhelmed with feelings, thinking about the incredible parallels between my life and those of the women CARE was helping. Dale was standing with me, and somehow Bob came up in our conversation.

"Do you know what it feels like to be erased?" I asked him. "To have someone try to turn you into nothing?" Dale just looked at me solemnly, and then he shook his head.

"Well, that's what Bob tried to do to me," I told him. And he had almost managed to do it too. But with the help of my own village of women, and my new husband, and my children, and these beautiful people from CARE, I was well and truly on my way back.

Even though the Middleburg town council had voted to approve our MOU for Salamander Resort, there were a few more administrative hoops to jump through before we could start construction. In the meantime, I had begun building an executive team, most of whom were now sitting around twiddling their thumbs because of the delay. So I decided it was time to make a move elsewhere.

Salamander would be our flagship resort, but I wanted to invest in other hotels as well. In 2006, when the Woodlands Resort & Inn in Summerville, South Carolina, became available, I decided to buy it. The main building was a hundred-year-old mansion that had recently been transformed into a luxury inn, and it sat on one hundred acres of Low Country land just outside Charleston. The whole property had a magical feel to it, and *Forbes* had designated it a five-star resort. But I wanted to take the Woodlands to another level. I sent my team down to refurbish and update the inn and grounds, and we added a lovely dining area called Pines.

It felt good to be launching my hospitality business, though so far, I'd just been laying out money in Middleburg and Summerville without a whole lot coming back in. You have to spend money to make money, and at the time, I wasn't too worried about it. In fact, in July 2007 I decided to look at acquiring another property—the Innisbrook Resort & Golf Club in Palm Harbor, Florida, just outside Tampa.

Rumor had it that the resort, which was owned by the Golf Trust investment group under Westin Hotels, wasn't in great shape. But the first time I went down there, I couldn't believe how shoddy it looked. This was a nine-hundred-acre property with four golf courses, including one that hosted a stop on the PGA Tour, the Tampa Bay Classic. Because Westin was struggling financially, the company had been unwilling or unable to keep the property in good shape.

Innisbrook had more than 750 employees, and on several trips down there, I tried to meet and talk to as many of them as possible. People were truly scared that the resort was going to close down and they were going to lose their jobs. Some of them had been working there their entire adult lives; Innisbrook felt like home to them and they were desperate to save it. When I told them I was considering buying the resort, a few of them actually broke down crying. I knew I could get it for a good price because of the shape it was in, and from a business perspective, it would be a smart investment. But what sealed the deal were those personal conversations with the people who worked there.

I bought the resort for $35 million, which was less than half of what it had been valued at just two years earlier. On the day of the announcement, I brought my whole Salamander executive team down to Innisbrook, and we gathered hundreds of employees in one of the ballrooms. We did a clap line, walking down the middle of the room while everybody clapped on either side, and the mood in that room was just as joyful as it could be. I got up on the stage and announced that we had bought the resort, and I mean, that place erupted. It was a love fest—and it still is, every time I go down there.

Fixing up the resort and its four golf courses was going to be expensive, that much I knew. We started renovations right away, expecting to spend between $20 million and $40 million to turn this into a world-class property. I became the only woman owner of a golf resort on the PGA Tour, and obviously the only Black woman. The US Golf Association invited me to join its board, and oh my goodness—it was me, one other woman named Diana Murphy, and then white men as far as the eye could see.

I ended up writing a memo for the USGA board, suggesting ways to get more people of color involved in their sport. I don't know whether they took my recommendations, but golf became just one more in a long line of traditionally white spaces that I wanted to try to integrate. From classical music, to equestrian events, to Confederate country, and now to golf, I was always drawn to places that Black people don't usually go. I liked the challenge of integrating those spaces—but more important, I wanted to open up possibilities for young people who might excel in places their parents and grandparents never got the chance to explore.

• • •

Meanwhile, as I was pouring money into Woodlands and Innisbrook, the estimates for how much it would cost to build Salamander Resort & Spa were skyrocketing. The US construction market went completely haywire in 2006 and 2007, and suddenly, the cost of building the resort was threatening to outstrip our ability to make it back.

"I hate to tell you this," Prem said to me one afternoon, "but one hundred twenty rooms won't be enough. It doesn't pencil out."

I just stared at him. We had gone from 40 to 58 to 120 . . . and now we'd have to ask Middleburg to approve even *more* rooms? "How many do we need?" I asked Prem. He told me that somewhere between 160 and 170 rooms would make the project feasible at the level of luxury I wanted.

"Or you could make some compromises," he said, his eyebrows rising. "You could make the common areas and restaurants smaller, or choose different materials for the structure or the interiors." If I cut some corners, he was saying, we could bring the cost down and keep the resort at 120 rooms. But even as the words were coming out of his mouth, Prem knew what my response would be.

"Nope," I said. "Not an option." If we needed to add more rooms to keep the quality up, we'd just have to add them, because I was not going to compromise on quality. So we decided to go back to the Middleburg town council one more time, to ask them to approve 168 rooms at the resort.

As fierce as our battle for approval had been in 2005, that 4–3 vote had broken the spell. The town knew that the resort was coming, and while some people were still opposed, there was no organized pushback to our request. By now, most people were excited about the new wastewater treatment plant and the tax revenues the resort would bring. On August 9, 2007, the town council opened debate, and five townspeople stood to comment—all of them in favor of supporting Salamander Resort. One of them, Sonnie Underwood, said, "The best thing to have in life is your family and friends. And I think that Sheila Johnson and the Salamander staff will be good friends to our town." The tide had truly turned.

The council voted 6–0 to approve the increased number of rooms, and it also passed a few other technical changes relating to zoning and permits. Five years after buying the Harriman land, we finally had full approval from the town and could start construction. I stood up at the end of the meeting with tears in my eyes and thanked the mayor, the council, the staff, and the residents of Middleburg for their support. "I will not let you down," I told them. And I invited them all to come and enjoy the resort whenever it was finished— hopefully by the end of 2009.

That prediction would turn out to be wishful thinking. Because almost as soon as we started pouring money into building Salamander, the Great Recession hit.

Building a luxury resort from scratch is an *expensive* undertaking. Before we even put a shovel in the ground, we knew it was going to cost in the neighborhood of $160 million from start to finish. I was paying for it myself, without investors—just like I was paying for the renovations at the Woodlands and Innisbrook. I was getting in deeper and deeper, trying to make my dream of a world-class hospitality company a reality. And then actual, present-day reality came clapping back.

With the sale of BET and receiving my half of the divorce settlement, I had felt pretty comfortable making these big financial commitments. But in the first half of 2008, the economy started to falter. The stock market, which had reached record highs in 2007, took a sickening drop. Rumors started flying that the housing market was a bubble that was about to burst. And I started to get scared.

In March 2008, Bear Stearns collapsed. Alan Greenspan predicted that we were heading toward the worst financial crisis since the end of World War II. That summer, the big mortgage company IndyMac collapsed. Then it was as if a dam had burst: In September, Freddie Mac and Fannie Mae failed, and Lehman Brothers declared bankruptcy. And on September 29, the Dow fell almost eight hundred points, the largest drop in the history of the market. The economy was headed toward disaster—and so were my nerves. I lost a lot of money in the stock market crash, even as the cost of all these renovations continued to rise. And of course, the luxury resorts I was spending all this money on weren't going to draw a whole lot of guests if the US economy truly collapsed.

With the economy falling to pieces around me, one of my vice presidents came to me and said, "Sheila, you are going to run out of money if we keep going like this." He went on and on about how dire the situation was, and how badly I was mishandling my money, and how I was going to end up broke. *Oh my god*, I thought. *After all this?* After fighting for those approvals, facing down the racists and naysayers, finally breaking ground, and getting halfway through construction, could my Salamander Resort dream actually turn into a nightmare?

Then I got a call from Jamie Dimon at JPMorgan Chase. I had a significant amount of my holdings in that bank, and as the economic storm clouds gathered, Jamie was calling some of his wealthier clients personally to discuss their individual situations.

"I'm sorry, Sheila," he said, "but I think you should mothball Salamander."

My whole body went cold. How could I just shut down the project with everything in full swing? I had contractors, builders, architects, designers, working 24/7 to create the resort. We were so close now—the building had been erected, and we were about to start working on the interiors. And *now* he wanted me to pull the plug on it? What was I supposed to do, just wrap it up in yellow tape and tell people we'd be in touch whenever the recession was over?

Unfortunately, that was exactly what he wanted me to do. I was terrified at the idea of it, but Jamie is the kind of person who can see over the horizon, so I had to trust him. We put a fence around the empty building, sealed up the windows and doors, and called a halt to all further construction activities. And then, we waited. For two . . . long . . . years.

Now, you can probably imagine what some of the local folks had to say about all this. Tongues started wagging quickly, with people going on about how "Sheila Johnson ran out of money," or "She's going to leave that thing half-finished," or "I hear she's going to sell it to Marriott, or some company in China." My resort building just sat there, a sad, empty shell, and I could hardly even bear to go look at it.

During that two-year shutdown, I truly didn't know what the future would hold. How could I? The entire world had been rocked by this meltdown, and no one knew what the global economy would look like on the other side of it. But I had to choose to believe—in the project, in my vision, and in my team. I was absolutely determined to open this resort, no matter what it took to make that happen. If I didn't, I would lose not only whatever I had invested in it, but also my home. There was no way I could stay in Middleburg if I'd fought for this, won it, and then never managed to get it open. I'd have to leave town with my tail between my legs and never come back.

One person who seemed overly interested in this distressing turn of events was—no surprise—Bob Johnson. As usual, he came swooping in full of opinions, telling me that I should cut my losses and partner up with the Four Seasons Hotels and Resorts, so they could take over the project. He probably wanted to get his thumb in the pie, and he also couldn't resist his usual habit of telling me what I was doing wrong, then insisting he knew the best way forward.

I told Bob I wasn't interested in the Four Seasons. I said that I knew what I was doing and had the project under control. I put on the bravest face I could muster. But inside, I was crumbling. Because everything that was happening was tapping into my oldest, deepest fears. I was in these three resort projects up to my neck, and I was scared that they were going to swallow me.

Once again, I found myself flashing back to my family's kitchen in Maywood, fifty years earlier. Hearing the EMT saying that I was going to have to pay $85 for my mother's ambulance. Realizing that I didn't have it and didn't know how to get it. Fearing that I was standing on the edge of a deep hole, about to fall in.

Emotionally, I was right back on the edge of that hole. I knew intellectually that I probably wouldn't end up in poverty, but that didn't matter. Deep down in my soul, I felt that same fear. And do you know what I did? I started putting coins and bills into piggy banks and storing them in different places in my house.

This makes no sense, of course. Piggy banks with a few hundred dollars weren't going to help if I blew through millions of dollars and actually found myself broke or in debt. But there was something comforting to me about having little stashes of a hundred dollars here, a hundred there. It helped to calm those deep feelings of insecurity.

At one point, while talking with my accountant, I said, "If I were to lose everything, at least I know how to sew." He just looked at me, not sure if I was joking or not. "I know how to wait tables. Or I could work as a caregiver," I said. "I have a lot of basic skills that I could use to earn money." He must have thought I sounded like a crazy person, but I am here to tell you that no matter how much money I have in the bank, I still think about this kind of thing *all the time*.

That's how strongly we're affected by the emotional traumas that happen to us when we're young. I can still summon the panic I felt in the kitchen that day, and it forever shaped the way I feel about money. Everything stems from that original moment—that original wound. And now, at age sixty, I was going to have to summon even more strength, one more time, to find my way past those feelings of fear and get my beloved resort built.

Fourteen

STARS AND DIAMONDS

Not long before the Great Recession shut down our construction, Robert Redford came to Middleburg for a visit. I'd met him at the Sundance Film Festival in January 2008, and we had hit it off right away. When I told him all about the resort I was planning, he decided to fly to Virginia and see for himself what we had going on out here.

I picked him up in the black Humvee I was driving at the time, and the minute he climbed in he was already giving me the side-eye. "Sheila," he said, "you *know* this is not an environmentally friendly vehicle." I'll be honest—I loved my Humvee, but getting called out by Robert Redford, with his long history of environmental activism, his gravitas, and of course, that amazing hair, definitely pulled me up short. "I know, I know," I told him. "I'll get rid of it, I promise." And I actually did, too, not too long after his visit.

We strolled around Middleburg together, and then I walked him up to the Harriman property. I was asking him about his Sundance

Mountain Resort in Utah, which he had turned into a must-see destination since buying it back in the 1960s. Like me, he had bought a spectacular piece of land that could have ended up filled with Mc-Mansions and condos, but Redford decided to "develop a little and preserve a great deal," as he put it. His resort was a huge success, drawing thousands of creative people out to his special place in the mountains, so I wanted to learn whatever I could from him.

But what he said surprised me. And then it excited me.

"This is a beautiful place, Sheila," he said, as we stood on the spot where the resort would be built and looked down toward Middleburg. Then he turned to me. "You should start a film festival here," he said.

Now, listen. When Robert Redford tells you to start a film festival—particularly when he's telling you this while standing on top of a windswept hill, with that dazzling smile on his face—you pay attention. What did I know about starting a film festival? Absolutely nothing. But I realized that if we did create one, it would bring creative people to our town and to Salamander, just as it had for Sundance. It would be a fantastic cultural addition to the area. And although it would be a lot of work, it would be *fun*. As soon as the words were out of Redford's mouth, I knew he was right. I talked to Prem about it, and by the time the recession eased and construction started back up, I was planning in parallel for a film festival that would launch when the resort opened.

A couple of years earlier, I had made my first foray into producing films when Ted Leonsis asked me to invest in *Kicking It*, a documentary that followed six people who played soccer in the 2006 Homeless World Cup. Colin Farrell narrated the film, which was directed by Susan Koch and Jeff Werner, and Ted produced it. I loved the idea of using a documentary to draw attention to the important social issue of homelessness, so I wrote a check to help get *Kicking It* made. In 2008, it was screened at the Sundance Film Festival, which is how I met Redford.

Giardy Ritz, my chief of staff, was with me at Sundance. When the screening finished and the audience burst into applause, I turned to her. "That's it, Giardy," I said. "I want to use *film* to make change." By that point, I'd been a CARE global ambassador for three years, traveling to dozens of countries to help women doing amazing work in difficult circumstances. I knew a filmmaker had started documenting the creative and inspiring ways in which these women were changing the world, so I decided to help fund that project too.

This would become the film *A Powerful Noise*. Director Tom Cappello followed three extraordinary women in Vietnam, Bosnia, and Mali as they worked to create positive change in their communities. Bui My Hanh, a young Vietnamese woman living with HIV/AIDS, founded a support group for others suffering from the disease, which was a source of terrible stigma in that country. In Bosnia-Herzegovina, Nada Marković created a raspberry-farming collective that brought together Bosniak and Serbian women. And a magnificent Malian woman named Madame Urbain fought for equal education for girls in her village. *A Powerful Noise* is a moving testament to the power of women, and it ended up premiering to rave reviews at the Tribeca Film Festival. Now I was really hooked.

Soon, Robert Redford asked me to join the board of the Sundance Institute, which I was thrilled to do. I produced a couple more documentaries—*Ella es el Matador*, about two female matadors in Spain, and *The Other City*, about fighting the HIV/AIDS crisis in Washington, DC. For *The Other City*, I did more than just hand over financial support. I went with the filmmakers to one of the roughest neighborhoods in town, where I spent a day providing needle-exchange services out of a van, giving clean syringes to drug addicts in exchange for their used ones. This was a surreal and sad experience, but it was inspiring too. For as much as I had traveled the world with CARE, here were people right in my own backyard who needed help.

The more deeply I got involved in making documentary films, the more excited I got about starting a film festival. I called Betsy Davis, who was now the mayor of Middleburg, and asked her to meet me at Market Salamander for a coffee the next morning. When we sat down, I said, "Betsy, I have an idea." I told her about my conversation with Robert Redford and said that I'd done some research and wanted to move forward with his suggestion. She laughed and said, "Well, Sheila, I should have known it wouldn't be a *little* idea."

I wanted the mayor's blessing, and she gave it. "I think it's absolutely great," Betsy said. "Even though I have no clue how you're going to pull it off."

Truthfully, I wasn't so sure myself. But I knew what we had to do to start: we needed to finally finish building the resort.

Even though I had told Prem I wouldn't compromise on the quality of what we were now calling the Salamander Resort & Spa, we did try to come up with creative ways to cut costs while keeping that quality high. And we came up with some surprising ways to do that.

Our plan was to have two large common-area rooms right when you walked in the front door of the building. One would be a spacious, airy, welcoming great room, with overstuffed couches, two roaring fireplaces, wooden coffee tables and end tables, and the feel of a grand old home. The other, the library, would be a cozy nook of a room, with dark wood walls, leather chairs, shelves of books, hunt-country art and knickknacks, and a more lived-in feel. Anybody could come and enjoy these rooms, whether they were staying at the resort or not. I wanted them to be a gathering place for people in town—Middleburg's living room.

As we drew closer to finishing the building, I decided to move furniture from my own house into those two rooms. Why not? I loved my furniture, and it was comfortable and reflected the cultural taste of the area. I wanted the resort to feel like home, and what better way to do that than actually bringing my home to it? That was the first step.

I also planned to display original artwork throughout the resort, from paintings and photography to sculptures, both indoors and out. And I wanted the art to reflect not only the local hunt-country equestrian culture but a more diverse array of cultures too. Although we were in the heart of the Confederacy, I wanted all guests—Black, white, brown, and everything in between—to feel not just comfortable but truly *at home* together. I wanted them to feel like Salamander Resort was theirs, a place to gather with friends, family, familiar faces. If we did it right, this would be one of the only luxury hotels in the United States that incorporated a specifically African American flavor in its design and décor.

But buying that kind of artwork—and particularly so much of it, since we now had to decorate 168 rooms plus all the common areas—is an expensive undertaking. So once again, I decided to look through my own house to see what I could come up with. For years, I had been collecting pieces by Black artists all over the world. From

Harlem to Kenya, and more recently on my travels with CARE, I had acquired sculptures, paintings, and wood carvings by local artisans. I gathered up these treasures and carried them down to the resort. I then chose where each piece would go—and I did the same for every other detail in the building, choosing everything from the wallpaper to the sconces to the carpets. I even designed the bed linens myself, getting them specially made.

Oh, and remember when Bob was so nasty to me about my photography hobby? Well, I never did stop taking photos, and a couple of years after I moved full-time to Middleburg, the Byrne Gallery on Washington Street mounted an exhibition of my work. At the opening reception, I was nervous, scared that maybe others would agree with Bob that I wasn't actually a photographer and was just being silly. But people packed into that gallery, perusing my prints of Italian landscapes, portraits of Maasai boys in East Africa, and even scenes from my own yard at Salamander Farm. We sold a few dozen prints for about $2,000 each, which reassured me that I *did* know what I was doing. So I decided to decorate Salamander Resort with my own photographs, which not only saved us money but felt *good*. Later, I also created a line of silk scarves imprinted with the images, and to this day, they sell like hotcakes in our gift shop.

Every single element that went into creating the Salamander Resort & Spa was deeply personal for me: Buying the Harriman land without having to ask anyone. Facing down the racist comments and "Don't BET Middleburg" signs. Pushing through the death threats. Finally winning council support and promising the town that I wouldn't let them down. Hanging on through the recession and the deep-rooted fear that I'd run out of money. And finally, pouring my heart and soul into every part of the design, every piece of art—every inch of space in that whole precious building and grounds.

When the worst of the recession had passed, and just before we resumed working on the resort, I invited Mayor Davis to come walk around the site with me. I liked Betsy, a down-to-earth woman whose family owned the Fun Shop boutique in town. She had three lovely daughters, one of whom my daughter, Paige, mentored when they were both at the Hill School. Betsy had always been supportive of me and of my projects in town, and I thought it would be nice to show her the progress we'd made on the resort.

I hadn't actually been out to the site in a while, as I'd been spending some time in New York working with the Parsons School of Design. So when I unlocked the doors of the still-empty building and we walked in, I found myself tearing up. "I'm sorry you've had so much to deal with," Betsy said, putting a hand on my shoulder. "The timing really was awful."

She was right about that, but as we stood in what would soon become Middleburg's living room, I said, "It hasn't been easy, but I am going to finish this." As we looked around, I could envision it all—the people, the art, the music, the laughter. It was only a matter of time now. Nearly a decade after buying the Harriman property, I couldn't wait for my vision to finally become a reality.

On Thursday, August 29, 2013, I stood on the front portico of the finished Salamander Resort & Spa. It was a spectacular, sunny day in Middleburg, and as I looked out at the hundreds of people who had gathered for our grand opening, my heart felt like it would burst.

Eleven years after buying this piece of land, through all the sweat and heartache and anxiety, we had finally done it! This was the proudest day of my life, and I couldn't wait to cut the ribbon, lead everyone inside, and show them what we had created.

So many people had come out to show their support. Friends, family, and neighbors in Middleburg. Mayor Davis and members of the town council. And we had some well-known folks in attendance, too, from other areas of my life. *Project Runway's* Tim Gunn and designer Donna Karan, both of whom I'd gotten to know while on the board of the Parsons School of Design, were there. Jackie Robinson's widow, Rachel, came, as did John Wall, my star point guard on the Washington Wizards. And David Gergen, who had become a good friend, not only came to support me, he also gave a beautiful speech.

David is one of the smartest people I've ever met, an adviser to four presidents and an incredibly astute political strategist. He's also the founder of the Center for Public Leadership at the Harvard Kennedy School, and a strong voice fighting for justice and equality in this country. David is white, but in his speech, he went right to the heart of what made Salamander extraordinary. He talked about how incredible it was for an African American woman to create this resort "at the foot of the Bull Run mountains," breaking barriers and opening up the area to a new diversity.

The day before, David had attended the fiftieth anniversary of the March on Washington, where the Reverend Dr. Martin Luther King Jr. had delivered his "I Have a Dream" speech back in 1963. He mentioned it in his remarks, then said, "Isn't it fitting that this week, fifty years later, we come to celebrate Sheila's dream? She will tell you it takes perseverance and courage . . . and she has plenty of both." Then he declared, "Somewhere up there, Pamela Harriman is smiling because of what Sheila has built with Salamander." Despite what Sam Huff had said at that council meeting eight years earlier, I'd like to think that Paul Mellon was too.

David then raised his hand for emphasis, looked around the crowd, and said, "I will guarantee you, the stars and the diamonds will be showered upon this resort." He meant that we would receive the highest ratings from places like *Forbes* and Michelin. But the image of stars showering down on my beloved Salamander brought tears to my eyes.

And then it was my turn to speak.

"Boy, what a day," I said. "I can't thank you enough for being here. This is the day we've all been waiting for." I had to stop for a moment, as the tears started to flow. "I'm pulling it together here," I said, then took a deep breath, trying to steady myself. "When we decided to mothball this project, I stopped sleeping," I told the crowd. "The recession hit us hard. But eventually my financial advisers said there was light at the end of the tunnel and that we could proceed."

My whole body felt flooded with emotion—I just couldn't believe this day had finally come. And I wanted everyone there that day to understand what this opening, and the support of this town, meant to me. "For me, this resort is personal," I said. "Middleburg was my refuge. In Middleburg I truly found serenity and friendship, and it is home. I want all my Middleburg neighbors to know that Salamander is your partner." Everyone started applauding, and then the whole crowd got on its feet. It was truly one of the best moments of my life.

My son, Brett, stood by me as we cut the ribbon, and I invited everyone to come in and tour the building and grounds. I can't even tell you how amazing it felt to welcome this beautifully diverse crowd of people, everyone from the old-guard white gentry to the Black friends and family who'd come from DC and its suburbs. We had a jazz band playing, and glasses of prosecco for celebrating, and the most delicious food from Chef Todd Gray. People seemed genuinely overwhelmed by what we had created. I had goose bumps throughout the whole thing, and a smile so big that by the end of the day my face hurt. It was everything I had dreamed about.

Of all the many people there that day, there are two I want to make special note of.

One was Bob Johnson. I didn't expect him to show up, but he did. And the look on his face was one I hadn't seen in a very long time, if ever. "Oh my god, Sheila," he said. "This place is gorgeous." I nodded, but he wasn't done. "You really did it," he said, a little smile on his face. "I have to hand it to you. You pulled it off." He seemed surprised, like he couldn't believe that I was capable of actually succeeding like this. What I wanted to say was, *I always could. You just never gave me the chance.* What I said instead was, "Thank you, Bob."

The most important guest that day, though, was my mother. By 2013, she had been in frail health for some time, and she had lived through all the ups and downs of the past decade right there in Middleburg with me. Even as she got weaker, eventually losing the ability to walk, her will to make it to our opening day grew stronger. "Sheila," she would say to me, "I am not dying until the doors of that resort open." She was absolutely determined, and part of me thinks that's what kept her alive for so long.

At the opening ceremony, she was right there with me in her wheelchair. She beamed throughout that whole day, rolling all over the property and telling everyone how proud she was of me. I was so grateful to have her there, this woman who had seen me through my worst times and had made it to seeing my best. When my life had crumbled, when I was down so far I didn't know if I'd ever get up again, she told me, "Sheila, you will get your power back." I wasn't sure I believed her then. But with her help, I had made it. And having seen that, she was now at peace. Just two and a half months later, on November 11, 2013, my mother died.

Just before she passed, my mother said to me, "Just think, Sheila. If you and Bob hadn't done BET, you wouldn't be here today. You wouldn't have this resort." I thought a lot about those words, and I knew she was right.

For as awful as that period was in so many ways, it enabled me to flourish over the last two decades in ways I'm not sure I would have otherwise. I really believe that in life, things happen for a reason. My mother was devastated by my father's leaving, but she found comfort in her community and happiness in her children and grandchildren. I was crushed by my father's actions, too, and they created a fear in me that led to bad decisions and insecurities that would upend my life. But they also instilled a fierceness, a determination to protect my own children, and a determination to succeed, all of which led me to where I am now.

I wouldn't want to live through that pain again. But the truth is, I wouldn't be the woman I am today if I hadn't gone through it.

I walked through fire and survived. I am the salamander.

EPILOGUE

As I write this, a decade has passed since that magical day when we cut the ribbon on Salamander Resort & Spa. I can hardly believe ten years have already gone by, in what feels like the blink of an eye.

The resort has become what I always hoped it would be, a place where everyone—Black, white, young, old, locals, and visitors from around the world—can come to relax, have a glass of wine, and spend time enjoying the surroundings. Salamander truly has become "Middleburg's living room," and the tax revenue and foot traffic we brought to the area have saved what was a dying town. Almost all the people who opposed the resort back in the early 2000s have come around, and many even apologized to me for having pushed so hard against it.

The one exception is Robert Duvall, who, as he promised all those years ago, has never set foot in the resort. It's a real shame, too, because I have no doubt he would enjoy it. And I would love to have him be an ambassador for the Middleburg Film Festival, now in its eleventh year and a major stop on the film festival circuit.

Amid that final rush to get the resort open in 2013, we also somehow managed to pull together a first-class film festival. Under the guidance of executive director Susan Koch, we were able to book and screen a full slate of amazing movies, including *Nebraska*, *August: Osage County*, *Philomena*, and *Lee Daniels' The Butler*. Showing *The Butler* felt especially sweet, not only because I was an executive producer on that film, but also because my husband, Bill, had a small part as a preacher.

Just as Robert Redford predicted, the Middleburg Film Festival has become a huge draw. We've had so many Oscar winners and Hollywood icons coming through, the *Washington Post* dubbed us the "itty-bitty Cannes." Film lovers have rubbed shoulders at Salamander with Emma Stone, Kenneth Branagh, Damien Chazelle, Dakota Johnson, Brendan Fraser, Maggie Gyllenhaal . . . and the list goes on and on. We've also had composers such as Terence Blanchard, Diane Warren, Mark Isham, and Michael Abels, who've performed to rapturous crowds. Music and the arts are what saved me as a young woman, and I feel incredibly fortunate to have a place where I can share them with others.

While the Middleburg resort will always be nearest and dearest to my heart, we also spent the last decade branching out into other properties. We took on the Aurora Anguilla and Half Moon Jamaica in the Caribbean, as well as the elegant Hotel Bennett in Charleston. In 2021, the Aspen Institute selected us to take over the Aspen Meadows resort—and let me tell you, I cannot wait to bring some *color* to that place. Then, in 2022, two amazing events happened.

First, we took over the Mandarin Oriental hotel in Southwest

Washington, DC. For the first time, "Chocolate City" has a Black-owned luxury hotel! What's even better, the newly christened Salamander DC is located just blocks from that first house I bought in Southwest all those years ago. Everything comes full circle. Not long after that, the *Washington Business Journal* announced that I was their "CEO of the Year." After all those decades of trying to prove myself, of fighting to be heard and appreciated, I feel extremely gratified to finally be recognized as a successful businesswoman in my own right.

I think of my life as happening in three acts. In the first, I was a young woman struggling to find her place in the world. In the second, I was a wife, a mother, a teacher, and an entrepreneur . . . and still struggling. But in this, the third act, I've discovered my true self—and with that, I've finally found peace and happiness. If I learned anything, it was that I had to close the door on the toxic part of my life before my heart could open enough to accept the good things that awaited me. Unfortunately, I had to hit the very bottom before I could start to climb out of that miserable place.

My journey here has been arduous, as you've read in these pages. But going through those awful times built my character and my strength. It also broadened my vision of how I wanted to grow my business and my philanthropic work. Over the last two decades, I've worked to lift up Black artists, producing Broadway shows such as *Thoughts of a Colored Man* and *Paradise Square*, and chairing events at the Metropolitan Opera in support of Black shows. I put fifty African American students through Harvard Kennedy School, a project suggested by my old friend David Gergen. I created Family Reunion, a three-day festival of Black American cuisine, which draws chefs from all over the country to Salamander Resort. When we gather there for three days of meals, music, and dancing, it truly does feel like family. And speaking of family, my beloved Washington Mystics, those hardworking women basketball players, won the WNBA championship in 2019. I nearly lost my mind with joy, celebrating with them that night.

My children, Paige and Brett, are both grown and married now, and I have two little grandbabies I adore. I wish my mother could have lived long enough to know them, but I take comfort in the fact that her spirit lives on through all of us. Bill and I are getting ready to celebrate our eighteenth wedding anniversary, and I love him more than ever. And you know, thinking about that number—eighteen years—reminds me of something I once heard about relationships.

People say that when you go through a breakup, it takes you half as long as the relationship lasted to get over it—so if your relationship lasted ten years, it'll take you five to start to feel right again. I was married to Bob for thirty-three years. And even though Bill and I got together not long after the divorce, I really struggled during those early years of our marriage. I still had nightmares, feelings of insecurity, even PTSD. While writing this book, I tried to think of the first time I felt truly happy and at peace. What popped into my head was a moment in Paris, with Bill.

The year was 2019. Bill and I had traveled to France for a party celebrating Patrick O'Connell, the chef at the Inn at Little Washington in Virginia, whose restaurant had just received its third Michelin star. We spent a week there, and there was something magical about it—and not because of anything fancy or out of the ordinary. Bill and I spent most of our time walking through the streets of Paris, stopping at little cafés for coffee and pastries, popping into art galleries, talking and enjoying each other's company. It felt like first love again, that flush of excitement and the happiness of simply being together.

Our hotel room had a view of the Eiffel Tower, which was lit up in bright colors for Fashion Week. One evening we just sat by the window, enjoying a drink and talking, and as I took in that magnificent view, my heart swelled. In that moment, I thought, *I'm okay*. I looked at Bill and said simply, "I feel truly happy, maybe for the first time in my life." I was at peace. I knew I was loved. And at long last, after a lifetime of second-guessing myself, I believed that I deserved it.

Sixteen and a half years had passed since my divorce from Bob. Exactly half the time we had been together. I was finally free.

If I could go back in time and talk to my younger self, I would tell her this: Trust your instincts. Get to know who you are before you give yourself to someone else. Believe that you can find happiness, and that you deserve it. You are going to be okay.

You are going to be okay.

Acknowledgments

To my husband, William T. Newman Jr., thank you for your unconditional love and for your support of this project. To my kids, Paige and Brett, I hope this book will inspire you as you move through life and continue to grow your families and careers.

To my best friend, Della Britton, thank you for always being there for me.

To my chief of staff, Giardy Ritz, thank you for the many years of blood, sweat, tears, and laughter. I couldn't do any of this without you. To the president of my company, Prem Devadas, thank you for continuing to help me fight the good fight. And to my executive assistant, Elena Roy, thank you for keeping the trains running on time.

To Susan Starrett, my teacher and mentor, thank you for always encouraging me to believe in myself.

To Jeff Lee, my brother from another mother: you are simply the best.

To Betsy Davis, thank you for believing in me and in my vision for the beautiful town of Middleburg.

To Sandy Ain, my confidant and lawyer, thank you for looking out for me.

To Bob Barnett, thank you for your always sage advice and for urging me to write this book. And to my friend Paula Robinson, thank you for encouraging me to tell my story.

To Lisa Dickey, my collaborator and now my friend, thank you for this therapeutic journey. I couldn't have done it without you (and those delicious martinis).

To Jon Karp and Dana Canedy, thank you for believing in my story. To my editor, LaSharah Bunting, thank you for helping me put it out into the world. To Maria Mendez and Priscilla Painton and everyone at Simon & Schuster, I am grateful to you all.

And finally, thank you to my mother, who picked me up off the floor when I was too far down to get up myself. I love you, and I miss you every day.

About the Author

SHEILA JOHNSON is an entrepreneur and philanthropist whose accomplishments span the arenas of hospitality, sports, television and film, the arts, and humanitarian causes. In 2000, she became the first African American female billionaire upon the sale of Black Entertainment Television, which she cofounded, to Viacom. Sheila is CEO of Salamander Hotels & Resorts, overseeing a growing portfolio of luxury properties, with her flagship property earning the coveted Forbes five-star rating. She is the only African American woman to have a principal shareholder stake in three professional sports teams: the Washington Wizards, Capitals, and Mystics, for which she serves as president and managing partner. She is the founder of the Middleburg Film Festival, dubbed "an itty-bitty Cannes" by the *Washington Post*, and she serves on the board of the Metropolitan Opera and is chairman of the College of Performing Arts at the New School. In 2022, she was named CEO of the Year by the *Washington Business Journal*.